AGAINST THE ODDS

Text copyright © Carmel Thomason 2014
The author asserts the moral right
to be identified as the author of this work

Published by
The Bible Reading Fellowship
15 The Chambers, Vineyard
Abingdon OX14 3FE
United Kingdom
Tel: +44 (0)1865 319700
Email: enquiries@brf.org.uk
Website: www.brf.org.uk
BRF is a Registered Charity

ISBN 978 1 84101 739 6

First published 2014

10 9 8 7 6 5 4 3 2 1 0

Acknowledgments
Unless otherwise stated, scripture quotations are taken from the Holy Bible, New Living
Translation, copyright © 1996, 2004. Used by permission of Tyndale House Publishers, Inc.,
Wheaton, Illinois 60189. All rights reserved.

Scripture quotations taken from the Holy Bible, New International Version (Anglicised edition).
Copyright © 1979, 1984, 2011 by Biblica (formerly International Bible Society). Used by
permission of Hodder & Stoughton Publishers, an Hachette UK company. All rights reserved.
'NIV' is a registered trademark of Biblica (formerly International Bible Society). UK trademark
number 1448790.
Scripture quotations taken from the New Revised Standard Version of the Bible, Anglicised
edition, copyright © 1989, 1995 by the Division of Christian Education of the National
Council of the Churches of Christ in the United States of America, and are used by permission.
All rights reserved.

Cover photo: Hemera/Thinkstock

A catalogue record for this book is available from the British Library

Printed and bound by CPI Group (UK) Ltd, Croydon CR0 4YY

AGAINST THE ODDS

TRUE STORIES OF FORGIVENESS AND HEALING

CARMEL THOMASON

CONTENTS

INTRODUCTION

The old law of an eye for an eye leaves everybody blind.
MARTIN LUTHER KING, JR

Growing up, I was taught by the adults in my life to play fair, yet time and again I learned through experience that life itself is not fair. Every day there is an opportunity to find offence or cause offence. However hard we try, we cannot control everything in life and we cannot escape hurt. As obvious as that seems, unfortunately it is not always clear what to do about it.

This book can't tell you how to forgive or give you a magic formula for healing. Just as in life, there is no one path that will take you there. Everyone's journey will be different, but there are things that can help you on your way. Some roads are longer than others, but you will discover from the testimonies given here that forgiveness is possible, and even in the darkest of circumstances you can find it.

The act of forgiveness does not sit easily with our natural instinct for justice; there is something both unreasonable and inexplicable about it. For this reason it is often easier to identify with those who can't forgive or who seek vengeance than to relate to those who have forgiven or strive for forgiveness in their relationships. Forgiveness is rarely, if ever, deserved, and that is why it is such a great gift. However, as these testimonies show, forgiveness is not simply a gift that we give to those who have harmed us. It is primarily a gift that we allow ourselves, a gift that can restore both peace and happiness in our hearts.

All the stories in this book are true and demonstrate some of the practical ways in which people cope in adverse circumstances. These actions help to bring them to a point at which the leap of grace that is forgiveness can occur. In similar circumstances, many other people might have become trapped in fear and bitterness, so what makes these people different? I hope you will discover that while some of their circumstances may be outside of your experience, these are ordinary people who have found the strength to forgive. What they have done is amazing, but you can do it too.

The book is split into two parts. The testimonies in Part 1 help us to explore the personal face of society's ills—war, crime and terrorism. The broad social issues covered in the first four stories are, thankfully, things that most of us only read about or hear on the news. For many people, these things happen to someone else, somewhere else. Yet behind each news item are individuals who feel they have lost everything, broken people who need to find a way to rebuild their lives.

You will read how these people pieced their lives back together. Of course, it is never as simple as forgiving one person and moving on. Joanne forgave her rapist but his actions meant that she had to rebuild her trust in strangers again, especially men. Penny, whose business was destroyed in a terrorist attack, had no individual to forgive, no perpetrator at whom to aim her anger. Both women had to learn, in different ways, to feel safe again in an uncertain world.

Sadly, despite the fact that World War I was labelled the war to end all wars, there are many conflicts still raging in the world today. Two of the testimonies in this book are from World War II, now more than a lifetime ago for most people. The men who fought have had many decades to reflect on what happened, and their stories reveal both the tragedy of war and the triumph of the human spirit. However, time is not, in itself, a healer. More than 70 years on, Ray has never stopped striving to help those who were captured alongside him in Burma to forgive. In Bill's case, his devastating injuries mean that he will carry the scars of war for the rest of his life. They are a constant reminder of the horror of war and meant that coming home was far from the end of his struggle.

If people who have suffered such terrible tragedy can forgive, why is it that so many of us, who never experience such pain, live in bitterness created by our own reluctance to let go of our hurt? The simple answer is that forgiveness, however big or small, is never easy, but the longer we hold on to resentment, the harder it is to let it go.

In Part 2 we hear everyday stories of forgiveness, which help us hold up a mirror and ask, 'Where are we keeping a record of wrongs against those we love or have loved, or even against ourselves?' Terry found that the pain of his divorce brought to the surface hurts from his past that he had kept buried for years. Consumed by anger and guilt, he has had to learn to forgive himself. Gary believed that his God could move mountains, but his world came crashing down when it appeared that the God in whom he had placed all his trust would not help. Through her marriage, Claire learnt the truth of Jesus' words to Peter that he should forgive his brother, not seven times 'but seventy times seven'. In the final testimony, after a fall-out with his brother, James had to face his pride and ask what was most important, being right or being loved.

In both parts of the book, each of the testimonies is followed by a short reflection, which is there to help you open a conversation about what you have just read. Do you agree with what has been written? Did you see something different in the story? If you are reading a story as part of a group, it might be helpful to jot down your initial thoughts individually, to share as part of a wider discussion. Each chapter includes a series of questions to help you to think about the wider issues raised. You will find that some of the topics resonate with your life more than others, but they may well be a start in helping you to think more widely about the benefits of forgiveness and how you can enjoy them.

All these testimonies are from individuals who have been generous in sharing their positive experiences of forgiveness, including the struggles they encountered along the way. Each story is told from one point of view. Of course there may be many points to consider, but, for us all, although we can try to look at life from another perspective, our own version of events is the one we live with. This is the individual's version and it tells us how they coped. Life is not always neat. You might not always agree with the way these people acted, and, by including these testimonies, I am not saying that theirs is the only way or even the right way to respond. It is their way, and you have to find your own.

The final chapter will help you to think about times when you have forgiven, how you did it and how it made you feel. There might be areas in your life where you need to practise forgiveness more readily. Perhaps there is a relationship that is suffering because of resentment caused by holding on to past wrongs, or pain that you had not recognised as being caused by a yearning to forgive. You might also be in a situation where you feel that you can't forgive. As forgiveness was one of the central teachings of Jesus, Christians can often feel guilty if they are unable to do so. If that is you, please don't feel guilty. Ask God to help you on your journey because, however bleak life looks, your story isn't over yet.

PART 1

Forgiving what seems unforgivable

I believe in the sun even when it is not
  shining;
I believe in love even when I feel it not;
I believe in God even when he is silent.

INSCRIBED ON A CELLAR WALL IN COLOGNE
DURING WORLD WAR II

1

SURVIVAL OF THE LUCKIEST: RAY'S STORY

How convenient it would be if we could blot out all the unpleasant things that have happened to us in life. Many of us will have a good try, but it is not possible to erase bad memories, not really. Would it be desirable even if we could? For if we forget the hardships and suffering we have experienced in life, then inevitably we must also forget the lessons learned from them.

We all have an incident or a period in life that we wish had worked out differently or had never happened at all—a time that had a profound effect on our lives, after which we can never be the same. For me it was the three-and-a-half years I endured as a prisoner of the Japanese. It was a long, hard road. We called it survival of the luckiest: I happen to be one of the lucky ones.

It was three years into World War II when my whole world was shaken by the fall of Singapore to the victorious Japanese army. Until that time, Singapore had been regarded as an impregnable fortress, but this myth was well and truly exploded by the Japanese in what was probably the greatest defeat in the history of the British Army.

I was serving in the Royal Corps of Signals in the British 18th Division and arrived in Singapore just two weeks before the surrender, barely one month after my 20th birthday. The final blow came on 15 February 1942 when the Japanese captured the MacRitchie Reservoir, situated in the middle of Singapore, which was the sole source of water for the whole of the island. After exploring all possible options, it seemed that, for us, the only answer was to give in.

As the order to cease fire trickled through, we hung around in disconsolate groups, disarmed and waiting for the Japanese to appear. We had all heard stories of atrocities, of Japanese fanaticism and their contempt for prisoners. Yet, whatever any of us thought at that moment, it didn't come close to the reality of the next three-and-a-half years.

We were captured as a division and marched together for 14 miles to Changi. On our way, Dick Sutton began whistling 'Colonel Bogey' and soon we were one big chorus. British soldiers had always sung derogatory and rude words to that tune and now seemed as good a time as any to use them.

I was grateful for Dick. Whatever the circumstances, he could always raise spirits enough to break a smile. Earlier in the war, we'd been billeted together at a wireless station dug out on a hillside above the divisional headquarters. Each day we would take it in turns to go into the valley to collect our meals, while the other remained on watch. One day I was walking back when a Japanese plane swooped down and began machine-gunning the road. I threw the dinners into the deep drain which had been hollowed out to accommodate the monsoon rains and dived in after them. There was nothing to do but keep low and pray that the enemy plane didn't return. Luckily it didn't, but my body was so filled with adrenaline that I was still shaking when I got back to the dug-out. I expected Dick to show concern and ask, 'Did he get you? Are you wounded? Are you hurt?' Not a bit of it. He just looked at me with a glint in his eye and said, 'Where's me bloody dinner?'

Unfortunately, this time there was no lucky escape and, once we reached Changi, it quickly became clear that we were in the hands of a ruthless and pitiless enemy. The Japanese had no concept of honourable surrender. In their view we had disgraced ourselves by not fighting to the death, and for this they held us in contempt. I hadn't surrendered. It was the general who surrendered, the rest of us were just acting on orders, but that didn't matter. Poor General Percival, he took the blame for all of it and it wasn't fair.

The Japanese didn't observe the Geneva Convention with regard to prisoners of war. Their guards roamed the camps, and we never knew when we would stumble across one, with dire results in many cases if we were not quick enough to jump to attention and bow. There could be a beating or torture at every turn—treatment not reserved solely for the prisoners. I saw a Japanese sergeant fell one of his own soldiers and gouge his eye out with the heel of his riding boot. The soldier's offence—coming into camp drunk and answering back.

Food rations were drastically reduced and were issued only for men who were fit to work, so, out of a camp of 1000, if 250 were ill, we were fed on rations for 750. It was rice or nothing. Breakfast was unflavoured rice gruel. For lunch we had a cake of boiled rice and there was a thin vegetable stew at night. If a bullock happened to drop dead in the vicinity, there was a chance we might find a faint trace of meat in the stew, but that was rare. Some men simply couldn't stomach rice: they starved and died. Others would trade their rations for cigarettes. Me, I ate it. Even when we were served up rice which had been limed ready for planting and boiled up into a green and glutinous mass, I still ate it. It was all there was.

Three months later, I was sent to Keppel Harbour to work on loading and unloading ships. Standing on the quayside, I had an uninterrupted view over the ocean. I can still close my eyes and picture the sunrise over that vast expanse of water. First there was thick blackness and then, gradually, a ball of fire would appear over the rim of the world, as it were, turning the sea momentarily blood-red. This was a sunrise more vivid and vibrant than I had ever experienced. It was a breathtaking and beautiful sight, heralding the glory of a new day and giving me fresh hope that I might live to see the next.

I stayed there until October of that same year, when I was one of a big party ordered to Thailand. It was rumoured that large camps had been established there, where we would spend the rest of the war in idleness and comfort, which for us spelt peace and tranquillity. For five days and five nights we journeyed north by rail, incarcerated in metal wagons which were like ovens during the day and refrigerators at night. There were 30 men to a wagon, many of them suffering from dysentery. Still, things would be better at the other side—or so we believed. Rumour was ever a lying jade!

The Japanese success in the Far East and, in particular, its rapidity surprised not only the Allies but the Japanese themselves, and they were faced with the problem that all advancing armies experience with rapid success. Their lines of communication became overstretched—too long and too vulnerable. The only way they could supply their troops in

Burma was by sea, a shaky business in view of the activity of British and American submarines. They needed an overland route, which would be safe from air attack because of their supremacy in that sphere at the time. The snag was that between Burma and the conquered territories to the south lay mile after mile of thick jungle.

Our job was to provide the solution by building a rail link through 400-odd kilometres of bamboo jungle to Moulmein in Burma. The route had been surveyed by the British before the war and abandoned as being too costly, both in economic terms and in terms of human lives. These factors, however, were no longer a problem for the Japanese. They got around the cost of raw materials by ripping up an existing line in Malaya, which possessed a railway along both east and west coasts: the Japanese decided that they didn't need both. As for human lives, well, they had us prisoners of war—a massive pool of slave labour that they viewed as an embarrassment and positively expendable—as well as the Chinese and Tamil labourers they treated as slaves.

So began the Burma–Siam railway or, as we came to know it, the railway of death—an enterprise which was to cost 393 lives for every mile of track laid.

We built our own camps. They were bamboo huts held together by rattan ties and roofed with palm fronds secured by strips of bamboo. Each hut would usually accommodate 200 men on platforms of split bamboo, ranged 100 each side. We made lamps out of cigarette tins filled with coconut oil, puncturing the lid to insert a piece of cloth for a wick. It doesn't sound too bad, does it? That's because I can't begin to explain the horror of it all. The huts were alive with bedbugs and lice. Latrines were trenches with bamboo slats across at intervals, on which we squatted. When the trench filled up, many a man weakened with dysentery would slip through the slats and tumble in.

Not that we spent much time at the camps—now it was work, work, work. We still had our British officers and worked under British Army discipline as well as Japanese. However, it wasn't long before everyone, irrespective of social rank or background, was reduced to the same abysmal level. Officers and men, we were all the same.

The railway was a lifeline to the Japanese. They depended on it to support their campaign in Burma, and so there was pressure not just on us but on our Japanese overseers to complete on time. From start to finish, the job was carried out with no mechanical aids worth mentioning. Every inch of jungle was cleared with axe and machete—trees felled, stumps dug out, ground levelled.

A three-foot embankment was constructed the whole length of the line. Every yard was built with earth dug out of the jungle with pick and spade, then carried to the site on rice sacks slung between two bamboo poles. Every sleeper and length of rail was manhandled into position and every securing spike hammered in by platelayers' hammers.

Bridges were constructed entirely of wood. Piles were driven into the ground by means of a primitive device we called a 'monkey'—a very heavy iron weight, hauled to the top of a massive tripod of tree trunks through a pulley operated by men at the other end of the rope. The weight would be released at the top to plummet down on to the pile of wood, hammering it into the ground. The operation was repeated, hour after weary hour, until the required depth had been reached.

On site, it was customary to identify the camp with a notice placed at the junction of the paths, so that parties passing through would know that a camp was near, should they require rest or water. One morning as we marched out to work, one notice read '9th Royal Northern Fusiliers Co. LT Col Flower'. When we marched back at night, some wag in the camp (most possibly Dick) had replaced it with one that read, 'This Way to the Flower Show'. It brought a lump to the throat, to think of sunny summer afternoons and village greens thousands of miles away—happier times.

I thought of my girl, Joyce. Would she know I was still alive? Would she still think about me, and would she care? I had to cling to the hope that she would. Having something to go back to was an incentive to fight. I'd seen men carried out to a prepared grave to be told by the medical officer, 'Now look, son, I've done all I can for you. The rest is up to you. You fight or you give in. If you give in, we put you in that hole tomorrow.' It was drastic treatment. Sometimes it worked and sometimes it didn't.

I remember the first real sorrow I felt at losing a close friend to war. It was shortly after I arrived in the Far East when I learned of his sudden and unexplained death. I had left him behind only a few short weeks before, and the news came as a huge shock to me and to all those in my close circle. Now death was everywhere—from cholera, malaria, dengue fever, dysentery, beri-beri, tropical ulcers, exhaustion, torture and hopelessness. I had become more hardened to it, but it still hurt. However desperate life became, living still mattered.

Uncertainty attended every waking hour. What would happen to us? In the midst of death and disease, would I be next? At times the spark of life burned feebly and all the ingredients were present for feeling that, if God existed, then he was doing a very poor job of looking after me. What kept me going was the hope of ultimate deliverance, sustained by the knowledge that one's misery was the result of man's sin, his inhumanity to his fellows, rather than to the indifference or non-existence of God.

I felt that God was there all the time, his love shining through the actions of men, one for another. He was there in every kindness, every act of compassion—it is how we survived. It was often said, 'It's every man for himself in here', but in reality nothing was further from the truth. We depended so much on one another for encouragement, morale-boosting and, in numerous instances, for our very survival.

We learned that God doesn't protect us from the hard knocks of life but, when we turn to him, he does give us strength to endure them. Through our confidence in God's goodness we found hope. Hope that someday the tensions and fears that were always present with us in the camps would be a thing of the past and we would return to a normal existence where we wouldn't forever be looking over our shoulders expecting a blow, or a Japanese curse, or both. Hope that we could start living again. When all other means of support and comfort were gone, hope kept us going.

The rail link was completed in October 1943 and, with due ceremony, a golden spike was driven into the ground to mark the completion. Not that there was much to celebrate. We lost 13,000 men building that railway, not counting the Chinese, Tamil and Malayan labourers whose lives were taken too.

Many prisoners of war were kept in Thailand to do the

maintenance work on the line, but my party was sent back to Singapore, from where we set sail for Japan. The convoy I travelled in got caught in action so we ended up fleeing and diverting to Saigon.

It was the monsoon season and we arrived at the camp at night in a deluge of rain. The weather was so severe, it was impossible to set up the cook house, which meant that even the measly rice rations were off the menu that day. With the moon as our only light, it was hard to see anything, but I heard singing and, looking towards the sound, spotted a large marquee which had been erected in the sodden ground. As I got closer I could make out the words: 'It's a long way to Tipperary...'

I smiled as I opened the tent to the sound of hundreds of British soldiers. I couldn't see a thing, but I didn't need to. Using what was left of my kit as a seat, I joined them, paddling in the mud. There we were, 'rolling out the barrel' and 'coming round the mountain', when a Dutch medical officer slumped down beside me.

'You British are mad,' he said. 'Here you are, cold, wet and hungry, without even the consolation of tobacco, and you are singing away as if you had not a care in the world. Tomorrow the sun will be shining, the cook house fires will be blazing, your tobacco will be dry and you will be grumbling and swearing—completely mad!' He paused before continuing, more to himself than to me, 'But I wish my Dutch boys were mad like you. I would take more of them home with me.'

We always said, 'It'll be over by Christmas.' Christmas would come and go and we'd start again: 'It'll be over by Christmas.' Eventually it was. For us, the hope was realised— we survived.

British, Australian and Dutch were blood-brothers bound together by a bond which had been forged in extreme adversity. We who had slogged through three-and-a-half years of privation and cruelty at the hands of the Japanese held a great service of thanksgiving for our deliverance. Several days after the service had taken place, Allied flags were hoisted over the camps—a great emotional moment. All went well until someone noticed that the British flag was flying a little higher than the other two, then all hell broke loose. Peace is such a fragile thing. At that moment I could only sympathise with the cynic who wryly commented, 'Blessed are the peace makers—they shall never be unemployed.'

We came out of captivity breathing fire and vengeance against the whole Japanese nation. All of us believed at that time that it would be impossible ever to forgive them.

Dick and I parted company when we landed back on British soil. The nightmare was finally over. Everyone made a tremendous fuss of us when we came back: there were people everywhere at Cardiff station and on the streets. I didn't know, when I stepped out of the train, if Joyce would be waiting for me. It had been almost four years with no word between us. Weighing seven stone, I was barely recognisable as the man Joyce had fallen in love with. I scanned all the faces. There she was—she did remember me! We married in September 1946. I couldn't do it earlier because I didn't have the money.

I settled back into civilian life very quickly, I think mainly because I had something to come back to. I didn't speak to Joyce to any great extent about what had happened. It was a horror story: there was no good repeating it in the family. All the same, my war-time experience was so tremendous that I couldn't just put it behind me, so to speak.

From the close bond forged in our adversity arose a network of clubs and associations under the banner of a National Federation with the avowed purpose, 'To keep alive the spirit which kept us alive'. By meeting, we were able to talk through our experiences and exchange views, keep up old friendships and make new ones.

At one reunion I met a fellow I hadn't seen since 1943, almost 30 years earlier. We recognised each other immediately and among the first words he said to me were 'I've not forgotten that drink of water.' Then I remembered a time when I stumbled upon him at the side of a jungle track where he had fallen, exhausted. I'd offered a mouthful or so of water which was left in my coconut shell water bottle, enough to revive him so he was able to continue, and together we completed the journey. We kept each other alive. Things like that, you don't forget easily. Yet for a long time the good was always tainted with the bad.

There was a lot of bitterness. As a Christian I was taught that we must forgive our enemies, but it took a bit of doing. I've always been a practising Christian, although the years in the camp made it difficult to carry out practical aspects like going to services. In 1977 I was ordained an Anglican priest and, as part of that, I felt that I had to preach forgiveness. Even years later, it was a taboo subject among our fellows and it wasn't an easy thing to get across because it was a lot to ask. More than one man has said to me after a sermon, 'It's all right, Padre, we'll take it from you because you were there.' It's hard to comprehend just how much there was to forgive, because there was no need for the sheer cruelty that was shown towards us.

I thought back to the time when we were 'rolling out the barrel' as our world crumbled around us. This picture of men who could be, and often were, cheerful under the most appalling circumstances is not an image of people who can let bitterness eat into their souls. Every instinct may be screaming at us to hate the Japanese guards for what they did, but we have to stifle this natural impulse, because in the world we hope to see established, there can be no room for hatred and vengeance.

The happiest people are those who can find it in their hearts to forgive. We need to learn from the past, not dwell on it. You can't breed peace on a diet of smouldering resentment, and if these thoughts are harboured in the minds of men, then your children or your children's children will be faced with the same problems, same dangers, same sufferings—except that they will be magnified beyond our comprehension.

One can't go on hating for ever, although some people might have a good go at it, of course. I can never forget what happened to me as a Far East prisoner of war, but the impact lessens as years go by. Time does heal the wounds, time does blunt the sharp edges of memory, and events that happened long ago become less stark and real.

Yet, for real peace, we need penitence—genuine sorrow for the mistakes and cruelties perpetrated in the past. All nations, without exception, are guilty here. And penitence involves protagonists coming together in a genuine attempt at understanding.

For the 40th anniversary of the war I returned to the Far East. I was invited by the Ministry of Defence to go as the chaplain to a party of widows visiting their husbands' graves. We were able to talk to the younger generation of Japanese, who were absolutely horrified at what we had to tell them. They couldn't understand their people behaving in the ways that they had. Of course, it wasn't all Japanese who had acted in that terrible way, but those who did were the only ones we knew.

At 89 years of age, I have enjoyed a span of life which I never expected to see. I was one of the lucky ones and many times over the years I've asked myself, 'Why?' The question is unanswerable: I simply don't know. Uppermost in my mind now is not bitterness but gratitude. I'm still never far from tears as I think of friends I served with and walked alongside in those far-off days of my youth. Yet there are many people who would maintain that sufficient time has elapsed to allow memories to fade, who see little point in memorial services. There are those who look upon Remembrance Day ceremonies as militaristic in nature, emphasising the glories of war. Of course, we who were involved know it is not true. No one who has personal experience of world war ever wants to see another one. There is no glory in war—just suffering, pain and tears.

People are only too willing to forget that war means prison camps, and prison camps mean degradation, starvation and death—not a glorious death on the battlefield but a slow death from ill-treatment, malnutrition and disease.

Yet, remembrance alone is not enough. For remembrance to mean anything at all, it must be accompanied by resolve— resolve that never again will men and women be subjected to the hardships and sorrows of war. From the peace of the grave our dead are entitled to say, 'Mark well how you use the time we gave you.'

While there is life and strength and breath in our bodies,

we should be striving for a better world, and our better world will come if the common people of the world wish for it and work for it hard enough. It's not so much celebrating a victory as rededicating ourselves to promoting peace and harmony among nations.

There are many I know who are moved to doubt as they look upon the mess that humanity has allowed God's world to drift into. We can prattle on as much as we like about the colossal waste of war. Everybody recognises this: no one in his right mind wants world war. We may differ in our opinions on the way to secure peace, but we all want it desperately. Yet the fact is, we still have wars.

If we are to lay the foundations of lasting peace in the world, there can be no room in our hearts for hatred. Some could regard this softening of attitude as a betrayal of our dead. I don't believe it is. We can still remember them with pride and gratitude, as indeed we do.

Peace within a person is where it all starts. It is a peace that can't be disturbed or broken by outside events. I do hope that you will strive for that inner peace, however you find it. The actions of nations are merely the actions of men writ large, and there are fewer of us left who were there to remind you of the depths to which a country can sink when hatred is allowed to fester.

I last saw Dick at Barnes Hospital in Gatley, Greater Manchester. He was laid down fully on his back and it was clear that he wasn't going to recover. As I approached his bed, I noticed that a biscuit had fallen on to his chest. 'Dick, you've dropped your biscuit,' I pointed out.

'Oh, I don't want it. You can have it,' he answered. Then all of a sudden it was as if life was filling him again. He lifted his head, grinned at me and said, 'We've seen the time when we would've snapped the bloody thing in half.' For me that's the essence of it all. We shared everything.

Dick died the next day. He was my great friend and, in the strangest way, having survived, I'm thankful for the time when we would have snapped a biscuit in half.

Reflection
The Rt Revd Dr Peter Forster, Bishop of Chester

Each of our lives began with what, from a human point of view, was a chance event—our conception in our mother's womb, when we were one among many millions of possibilities. From such a perspective we might simply say that we were lucky to be born.

Life continues to be lived in the context of luck and chance—what our genes dictate in our life chances, whether we suffer from a life-threatening illness, what other people do to us by accident or design, and so forth.

Ray Rossiter's story, aged nearly 90, brings all this home with a peculiar sharpness. He had the extreme ill luck to be a prisoner of the Japanese, and he was, as he puts it, one of the lucky ones to survive and, indeed, subsequently to flourish.

We live in a world that courts the myth of control, the belief that we can remove or, at least, largely mitigate the changes and chances of the fleeting world, as the old Prayer Book puts it. As I write, governments are struggling with the reality that we are unable to control events to the degree that had been anticipated, whether military campaigns in Afghanistan or monetary union in the Eurozone. Sooner or later, individuals and countries alike need to face the reality that we are not in control but are subject to all sorts of forces that are outside our control.

Ray's story is a sharp reminder of all this, writ large in the pages of the most extravagant war the world has ever seen, but none of us knows what is around the corner, what suffering and sadness we may personally have to face and endure.

Ray ends with the brief remark that 'in the strangest way' he is nevertheless thankful for the experience he shared with his fellow prisoners. 'Pain,' said C.S. Lewis, 'is God's megaphone.'[1] Life is a school for wisdom, and the challenge is to learn the wisdom of life when life seems most under threat, just as married couples learn most from what their vows 'for better, for worse' actually mean in practice.

Seen in these terms, for all the horror that was involved in his experiences, Ray's account can be an encouragement to us all as we make our way on life's journey. Our sufferings may involve only the foothills of comparable human experience, but at the end of the day we are all on a common journey.

What do you think?

- The sufferings and privations that Ray endured would have killed many a man. What do you think it was that helped Ray to survive?
- Where did Ray find evidence for the existence of God in the middle of such cruelty and inhumanity?
- In what ways does forgiveness benefit the forgiver and the forgiven?
- According to Ray, what are the benefits of services of Remembrance?
- C.S. Lewis said, 'Pain is God's megaphone.' If we are open, what lessons can we learn from the experience?
- What role did friendship play in Ray's experience?
- Ray says, 'Peace within a person is where it all starts… The actions of a nation are merely the actions of men writ large.' Do you think that an individual can influence the cause of peace in a positive way?

2

THE BEST
OF THINGS:
BILL'S STORY

Sometimes, when I stand on the beach opposite my house, it is almost as if the years are momentarily wiped from my mind. As the wind blows, carrying the unmistakable smell of seaweed, I feel a security in knowing where I am. In my head I'm a child again, enjoying the sun, sand and sea, with no thought for the future.

I have no idea of my appearance or how other people see me. The last time I saw my face in a mirror I was 21 years old, and I dare say that I have changed in the 70 years since then. It was 1942, the world was at war and I was stationed in the Far East, serving my country as First Class William Griffiths, RAF Transport Driver.

We had set out to rescue 200 stranded RAF men and ended up being herded into lorries as prisoners of war under Japanese rule. When the doors opened, we were ordered out by the side of the road, where there were about 20 guards, all with rifles and bayonets, shouting and gesticulating. None of them spoke English but, when one of them pushed me forward, it was obvious what he meant: I was to clear away the netting in front of me or get a bayonet in my guts.

Instinctively I knew it was deadly or he'd have done the job himself. I can't deny I was scared stiff, but what choice was there? I took the netting into my hands, noticing that the guards stood well back. They knew that it was covering an ammunitions dump, and I was about to find out.

My gentle tug set off a live grenade and I was hurled backwards in the explosion. I felt for my face—nothing. 'God, my face has been blown off!' The words rushed out as a desperate cry and, at the same time, a fleeting thought questioned how I could still speak if my face had gone.

I tried to get up and walk, but my right leg wouldn't support me and I fell. The pain was excruciating. Everything was black and I couldn't see what was happening, but I heard a truck pull up and English voices of men who lifted me into the back of it. Suddenly I felt terribly cold, like I was being lowered into a vat of icy water. Although I wasn't aware of it, I was losing a lot of blood.

The pain in my arms was unbearable. Death by bayonet began to seem the more attractive option as I pleaded to anyone who could hear, 'Please, put me out, for God's sake put me out!'

'All right, my boy, we will,' a calm voice replied, and I slipped into a merciful oblivion.

My short-lived respite was thanks to the effects of an-aesthesia on the operating table where Lieutenant-Colonel Edward 'Weary' Dunlop of the Royal Australian Medical Corps worked for more than two hours to save my leg, remove the remains of both of my eyes and tidy the stumps that were left of my arms. By rights I should have died of those injuries, and some might have thought it kinder to let me. Yet, for Colonel

Dunlop, when so many lives were being lost around us, even a flicker of life such as mine seemed too precious to let go.

When I gained consciousness, my right leg was in plaster from foot to hip. I knew my hands had gone, but I didn't realise that I'd lost my sight for ever and, sensibly, the hospital matron, Mickey de Jonge, didn't tell me.

'It's no good,' I pleaded with her. 'I can't spend the rest of my life a complete wreck. Give me an injection—something, anything. Just let me drift away. I can't accept being like this, I can't!'

'I would do it,' she comforted me, 'but I need Colonel Dunlop's permission. I can't do it without.'

I don't know if Mickey ever asked him, because each time I brought it up she would make excuses. Even if she had asked, I knew it was unlikely that Colonel Dunlop would agree. For reasons I couldn't fathom, he seemed to have taken a particular interest in my recovery, visiting my bedside regularly, despite having almost 1400 other patients to attend to.

'Don't you worry, my boy,' he reassured me. 'The Japanese will soon be defeated and, once home, your excellent constitution will see you through.'

I was unconvinced. In addition to my disabling injuries, the explosion had left my face speckled with powder burns and my body peppered with countless small pieces of shrapnel. The job of removing them was given to RAF Officer Andrew Crighton. He was a good choice. Andrew had a quiet, soothing voice and a gentle touch to go with it. Every day he would come along with his tweezers and prod and pick at my well-punctured frame to nip out fragments of metal. I trusted him and so I confided how hopeless I felt, certain that he would understand my need to be put out of this misery. He didn't.

'You can't be thinking like that. You'll be right soon enough,' he said, refusing to be drawn any further into my morbid conversation. 'Once you're home you'll get artificial limbs and, as for being blind, well, I know folk who are blind and they get along all right.'

Blind? Andrew used the word in such a matter-of-fact way, as if everyone knew that my sight would never return. Everyone, that was, except me.

Blind. Well, if I'd had any hope of recovery, I didn't any more. Far from the comfort he'd intended, this information only made me more certain that the sooner my life was ended, the better. Not that I could do anything about it. Even if, by some miracle, I could find the right drug to finish me off, I couldn't get it to my mouth. Both hopeless and helpless, what good could I possibly be to anyone?

For me, there was no life worth living any more, and nothing anyone could do or say would make me feel differently. Yet willing myself dead didn't make me so, and I was still alive a month after the explosion when the Japanese demanded the immediate break-up of the hospital. Like so many happenings in that dreadful war, the move was violent and sudden. In all of the chaos, Colonel Dunlop was determined I shouldn't become a victim of its savagery, risking his own life by standing between me and the bayonets of Japanese guards who regarded me as expendable. Again I was given the chance to live, whether I wanted to or not.

If I'd believed that life couldn't get any worse, I was about to be proved wrong. I was separated from Colonel Dunlop and all those who had done most to help me through those first weeks, bundled on to a stretcher and put on the back of a lorry for the journey to Tjimahi.

They called Tjimahi a hospital, but it was a prison. Fortunately there were several Dutch, Australian and British doctors, but all the nursing had to be carried out by fellow prisoners. I was allocated Joe Holland, a soldier of my own age who came from Burnley, quite close to my home town of Blackburn. Our common past gave us plenty to talk about, and we would natter away while Joe fed me rice, which was about all we ever had to eat.

I learned that Joe had been a postman in civvy street and, in turn, I told him about how I'd joined my grandfather's haulage business at 14, and how much I had looked forward to passing my driving test at 17 so that I could drive a lorry myself. I'd travelled all over the north of England, then up to Scotland and down to London. Driving gave me such freedom and it was a useful skill when I was conscripted. Talking about those times made me realise how much I missed my life back home and how much I wanted to keep it alive, if only by chatter. I was also aware that I hadn't given a thought to my wife or little girl since I'd been wounded. I'd been cut off from any life I knew, in a world of blackness and pain. Now, as I dreamt out loud of another life, a better life, the feeling of despair that had hung over me for so long began to lessen.

We'd been in Tijmahi for about six weeks when a Dutch doctor suggested that it was time to remove the cast from my leg. 'Excellent, excellent,' he pronounced as he inspected my leg, which was a little shrunken and wrinkled but healed nonetheless. 'In one week you must try to stand on it a little.'

For once, the worst hadn't happened. When the time

came, with Joe's help I swivelled myself round, got my good leg over the side of the bed, then the damaged one, and heaved myself on to my feet, where I tottered for a moment before collapsing back on to the bed. This wasn't going to be easy but, having tried once, I had to keep going.

The next day I managed to creep around the bed and into the other side. The old leg was holding up well and, once I'd begun to get a sense of balance again, I found the confidence to cast off from my bed and try walking up the ward, using my arms as bumpers, which hurt less than my nose. I didn't get very far the first time and suffered a few knocks in the process, but at least I was able to have a chat with some of the other patients who, up to that point, had only been voices in the distance.

Whatever subject the conversation started on, we nearly always ended up talking about food. We complained about the lack of it and tormented ourselves with recollections of the most delicious meals we'd had in the past and what feasts we would have back home. Sharing stories with the other men, I soon realised that I wasn't alone in this horror. We were all hungry, frightened and weary—and I certainly wasn't the only one who'd been maimed. An Australian prisoner told me that he'd had most of his face blown off and was terribly burned.

'I've just looked at myself in the mirror and my face is a right mess,' he remarked one day. 'Reckon my wife'll throw me out when she sees me. You're lucky in one way, Billy. At least you can't see yourself.' I laughed for the first time since the explosion, and it took me completely by surprise that I could.

Blind or sighted, whole or maimed, we were all in the

same boat and all had a job to keep our spirits up. From then on I resolved that, however full of despair I might feel, I would do my best not to show it. As far as I could, I'd put on an air of cheerfulness, whistling and singing as I wandered around. That way, I felt, I might have a part to play in helping others. To add to my resolve, news arrived that Colonel Dunlop was in one of the camps at Bandoeng. Hearing his encouragement, from patients who had been transferred from Bandoeng, was a tremendous source of strength. I owed it to him to go on living and to make the best of things.

Although everyone, including me, at one time or another went down with the usual tropical illnesses—dysentery, malaria and dengue fever—I did my best to keep fit. Every morning, if I wasn't actually ill, I would do my exercises, touching my toes with my stumps (which meant bending down a lot further than simply touching them with finger-tips), running on the spot, knees bend, stre-e-e-tch, and others I'd learnt doing physical training in the RAF.

Some of the prisoners made me a holder, from old tin cans smuggled into the camp, so that I could carry a stick, and another to hold a spoon so that I could feed myself. They were a tremendous boon but, as soon as I began to move around the camp, I became as much of a target for the ruthlessness of the Japanese guards as anyone. They had a habit of stopping me, shouting or giving me a clout, probably because I didn't bow to them as they insisted every prisoner should. It wasn't out of arrogance, or resistance. I simply couldn't see them, but they didn't care.

Guards would come and tickle my feet or throw leaves and twigs into my face as I was walking, snatch my stick, prod me with their bayonets and spin me around. I think they thought it was a joke. Oddly, I was rarely scared. Perhaps it was because, deep down, I didn't care if I lived or died—or so I thought, until a Japanese guard held a rifle to my chest and asked, 'You want die?'

My response was an emphatic 'No!' while shaking my head to make it perfectly clear.

'No eyes, no hands, you better dead!'

I shook my head again as the guard pressed the muzzle of his rifle against my heart, shouting, 'You better dead!'

Deep down, there must have been some fight left in me, because while I was most certainly still miserable, I realised that I no longer wanted to die.

I lived that way for three-and-a-half years, until the day finally arrived that we had all been dreaming of. The war had ended and it was time to leave Java. There weren't many outward signs of excitement among the prisoners. I suppose our resistance was low and we simply didn't have the emotional energy to respond to our change in fortunes. On hearing the news, I went back to my bed and lay there thinking about my future. I was now free, so why did I feel so scared, confused and utterly weary? I had so longed for captivity to be over and had comforted myself many times with the dream that once I was home again, somehow I would be all right. But how could I ever be all right again? Even if I wanted to forget this war and all that had happened during it, my battle scars would be a constant reminder. The war had ended, I was liberated, but what was beginning for me now?

Anxiety stayed with me as I boarded the hospital ship in Singapore, ready for the long journey home. I couldn't help reflecting sadly that I was a very different person from the carefree, adventurous lad who had arrived four years earlier. Was my life from now on to be nothing more than remembering the past—what my life was like before I came to this place, a life when I could touch and see?

Soon after we set sail, I received my first letter in nearly four years. A friend read it to me. It was from my Uncle Robert, who had taken over the family haulage business after my father died. I told myself that he had written because he was now the most senior member of the family, but I did wonder why there wasn't a letter from my mother.

My uncle's note was brief. He would meet me at the port, and when I got home my mother would look after me for a while, although it would be hard for her.

The journey home gave me two months to brood on the absences in that letter. I tried not to worry and clung to the knowledge that, at least, there would be the family business to come back to—a haven in which, even though I should never be able to drive again, I could at least be useful in the office and get an occasional run on the old familiar routes as a driver's mate. I was, after all, the eldest son, and as such I had a right to take my late father's place—or so I thought.

Once off the ship, I could hold on to my dreams no longer.

'Billy! It's your Uncle Robert. How are you, lad?'

'Not too bad, Uncle.' There was a pause while the ambulance men were fussing round, wanting to be off.

'They're taking you to the RAF Hospital at Cosford. I'll come with you.' There was another pause. 'You don't look too bad at all. A bit older, perhaps, and a lot thinner.'

'I expect I do.'

'It's been a long time,' my uncle said as we clambered aboard. We were both embarrassed and awkward with each other, and, while it was nice of him to come to meet me, I wished he hadn't bothered.

'How's mother?' I asked.

'She's fine.'

'And the business?'

He hesitated for a second, and then said casually, 'Oh, that's been sold up.'

I couldn't quite take it in. 'What happened? Why was it sold?' I stammered.

He muttered something about war-time difficulties, fuel rationing and the Ministry of Transport. 'As a matter of fact, I've started up my own haulage business, doing much the same kind of work as the old firm. It's going pretty well,' he said cheerfully, before changing the subject to the generous pensions and allowances I should get and how I would be looked after.

Nothing made sense. What had been going on while I'd been away?

'I have to tell you—' His voice was hushed. 'Ethel, your wife. I'm afraid she's hooked up with someone else; had a baby by him, I hear. But your kid's OK. Ethel's sister has taken her on and she's doing fine. I dare say it's all for the best.'

There was an awkward silence. Perhaps he hoped I'd fill it, but with what? I had no reply. No words could ever reflect how I felt about what I'd just heard.

'You'll be all right, lad, I'm sure of that.' His voice was loud and confident. 'Your mother will look after you and there's St Dunstan's, that charity what cares for blinded servicemen— they'll help. You'll not be left to cope on your own.' With that, he patted me on the back and headed back to Blackburn, leaving me in the hands of two Women's Auxiliary Air Force nurses and an orderly, who undressed me and whipped me into bed like I was some kind of invalid. I had a feeling they were all wearing masks, as if I had the plague or something. Perhaps I did—the plague of disability.

It was clear that no one had expected me to come home. I was worried about what my mother's reaction would be when she saw me, but it was all right. She hugged and kissed me, then, with a kind of sob, said, 'You're so thin, Billy,' as if all she wanted was to get a good feed into me.

While I'd been away, my mother had remarried a watchmaker, also called William, and was now Agnes Walmsley. I had not known my new stepfather before they married, but he was a patient, easygoing sort and we got on well. I'd sit quietly in the corner of his workroom, we'd exchange the odd word, then I'd hear him push back his chair and get up. 'Well, Billy, what about a walk?' he'd say. Helping me into my coat, he'd take my arm and we'd potter off together to the local park, chatting about the changes that had taken place in the town and about people we both knew. I enjoyed getting out, and my stepfather never seemed to mind taking me or make me feel like it was a chore for him.

I'd grown up in the town. I knew every road and street and could picture in my mind the exact route we were taking. Once or twice a week my grandpa would come to walk with me, too. Grandpa had been born with a withered arm and this made him all the more sympathetic and understanding towards me. 'It hasn't made life any easier having only one good arm,' he told me, 'but I managed and so will you.'

It was nice to be encouraged, but I didn't have the slightest hope of managing by myself. The mechanical hands that would change everything, or so I'd been promised, weren't the miracle I'd expected. They felt very heavy and the only moving part was the thumb, which flicked in and out like a crab's claw.

'They look all right, my boy,' my mother said, but I could feel the bitterness and disappointment welling up in her when she saw how limited the movement was and how little I would be able to do with them. If she had accepted my situation more readily, perhaps I would have felt less miserable, but my mother was not the type to take disaster in her stride and it soon began to affect her health.

To ease my mother's burden, the local St Dunstan's Welfare Officer suggested that I have a spell at Ian Fraser House, Ovingdean, near Brighton, the charity's rehabilitation and training centre. I wasn't sure that I liked the idea of rehabilitation and training. It sounded like some kind of institution and I'd already had a belly full of that. Nevertheless, after some persuasion, I reluctantly agreed. After all, whether I went or whether I stayed, it seemed to me that I would still be the same useless wreck and a burden on whoever had to look after me.

On my first morning at the centre, the head of Ian Fraser House, Air Commodore Dacre, invited me into his office for a chat. 'Don't worry if you feel nervous or frustrated. That's only to be expected,' he reassured me. 'What you need is time and rest. It's our job at St Dunstan's to help make your transition back to normal life as smooth as possible. Let's take this one step at a time. There's no need to start thinking about the future just yet.'

Since I'd heard that the war was over, worrying about the future was all I'd seemed to do. To be told not to worry about what might become of me lifted a great weight from my mind. It was exactly what I needed to hear, especially coming from Dacre. During the First World War he had been a prisoner of the Turks and, although he said that they were nothing like as bad as the Japanese, they were not the gentlest of captors.

Far from being the institution I had feared, St Dunstan's gave me a feeling of freedom and I was pleased that the officer had been so persistent in encouraging me to visit. From the main entrance, railed paths down to the seashore, the sports ground and the bus stop enabled me to wander about alone. Being able to go out for a walk without waiting to be asked gave me a great sense of independence. I tried to imagine St Dunstan's building, like an ocean liner, staring out over the sea. They say that if you look across the water on a clear day, you can see the Isle of Wight. Although I couldn't see the magnificent views, I could smell the clean tang of the English Channel and hear the waves crashing on to the beach. I knew the scene was beautiful. Whether or not my mental pictures bore any relation to the reality was immaterial.

Being able to get around freely stopped me worrying about keeping fit, something that always bothered me, even more so since the explosion. At St Dunstan's they had terrific gadgets that enabled me to throw a javelin, put the shot and take part in ten-pin bowling. I'd never imagined that I'd be able to play sports again. I wasn't brilliant or wonderful at any of it. I'd just take part for the fun and do the best I could.

My time at St Dunstan's was a revelation. While there, I learned to play the trombone, using a gadget that, when fitted to the body of the instrument, enabled me both to hold the mouthpiece to my lips and to move the slide in and out. More valuable than that, I learned how to type, using a metal rod strapped to the stump of each arm and a specially adapted typewriter. It took many months of patience to master, but I realised that to be able to type would be a tremendous advantage, so I persevered.

Of course, none of these new skills came easy, but although they may have been difficult they were not impossible, as I had believed before. Blind and without hands I might be, but there was still life in me which was more than a mere existence. I could walk and talk and hear and enjoy the company of friends, and, who knows, I might still find something worth living for.

From time to time, Air Commodore Dacre would call me into his office for a chat to find out how I was getting on. On one of these occasions I happened to mention the family haulage business, and how desperately I'd hoped to be able to take part in it when I returned from the war, but that everything had changed in my absence and now there was no place for me.

Dacre paused for a moment. 'Ever thought of starting up on your own, Billy?'

'My own haulage business, you mean?'

'Why not?'

'Do you think I could, like this?' I said, raising my stumps as if my disability needed emphasis.

'It's worth thinking about,' he said positively. 'If you're interested, leave it with me and I'll make some enquiries and let you know what I find out.'

My head was buzzing. Could I possibly manage it? Was it even possible? I was completely out of touch with conditions in the industry, though I did know that getting a licence to operate was by no means easy. Every application for an 'A

Licence' was automatically opposed by other hauliers and by the railways, who resented the competition. Even supposing I could get over that hurdle, I'd have to buy a lorry and employ a driver, but with what? Where would I get the money from?

The questions hammered around in my head, and with the questions came the old fears. I knew all too well what living at home was like, whereas here at St Dunstan's I was happy and relaxed, surrounded by friends and by staff who were experienced and understanding.

As I weighed up the pros and cons, I regretted ever having mentioned the business to Air Commodore Dacre. At the same time, I knew in my bones that if I didn't accept the challenge, then I would regret it for the rest of my life.

The problems I'd worried about weren't as insurmountable as I first thought. St Dunstan's agreed to lend me the money to buy a vehicle and the Air Commodore put me in touch with a man who was not only well acquainted with the transport industry but also knew all about business management and book-keeping. I spent a number of brain-stretching hours under his tuition and, as the months went by, I realised that what had started off as a whimsical idea was becoming a reality.

I had the necessary rudimentary skills to enable me to run the business, I had the finance to buy the vehicle and my two brothers agreed to come in with me as driver and mate. Finally there was no turning back. I decided to leave Ovingdean and return home to start my great adventure.

William Griffiths, Blackburn, began operating in January 1947. The office was my room in my mother's house. I had a typewriter and a specially adapted telephone, which enabled me to run the business. We couldn't afford the luxury of a secretary, but I did have a young chap who came in for a couple of hours each week to do the books. My contribution was to arrange jobs by telephone, to keep customers happy by ensuring that the lorry was in the right place at the right time, and to soothe them if they phoned up in an irate mood to complain that a lorry load hadn't arrived when it should have, or hadn't been collected on time.

To be involved with other people, to be part of the community and to have a job to do was a great thing. I think we may still have been on the road today were it not for the nationalisation of road and rail transport later that same year. It was some time before the full effects of the government's bill hit me. I managed to keep going through 1948 and into 1949, but when the business eventually failed it was a heavy blow.

To help pass the time, I would listen to the radio, and when the radio failed me I would rig up my trombone and have a good blow on that. On the face of it I was back to square one, but inside I didn't feel the same. I'd only failed because the rules had changed. The experience had taught me that I was able to do a useful job, if only I could find the right one.

The worst part of having nothing to do was feeling housebound, because, unless someone offered to take me out, I was stuck at home. Luckily I'd made the acquaintance of an ex-service chap by the name of Sid Wilding. Sid was a lively, outgoing type who had served alongside Frankie Howerd in his Entertainments National Service Association days and knew him well. He was a bit of a comedian himself and often took part in the club shows, singing a song or telling a few jokes.

Sid's cheerfulness and kindness were a real tonic for me.

He would call at my house two or three nights a week and we'd go out together, sometimes to the pub and sometimes to the working men's club, where there would always be a show on of some kind.

One night, while Sid was at the bar, I heard a woman's voice. 'Billy, this is Ivy Walkden. You won't remember me, but you might remember my niece, Alice Jolly.'

'Of course,' I said, smiling at the memory of those days before the war. 'I remember Alice very well. She tried to teach me to dance in the old days.'

'That's right,' she laughed. 'She's a concert singer now. She must have forgiven you for stepping on her toes because she says she'd like to see you again. I was talking to her only yesterday.'

'Great! I'd love to meet her again.'

I remembered Alice as full of life and fun. A whole crowd of us used to go about together. We'd been jokey, light-hearted kind of pals, and it would be nice to meet again. But… there was always a 'but…'. What would Alice think when she saw me? Obviously she'd know what to expect, but that wasn't the same thing as being faced with the reality.

The following week, good to her word, Ivy Walkden picked me up and took me to tea at Alice's. All the worry about what Alice would think of me disappeared as soon as she spoke. As we laughed and joked about old days, there was no recoil or tension in her voice, only a warmth and friendliness that I'd hardly known during all those years. It wasn't the compassionate warmth of pity, but the other kind that normal people feel towards each other, liking and affection, on equal terms. How much I'd missed that and how badly I needed it.

As I was leaving, Alice said, 'Why not come to one of my concerts—you and Sid?' I was afraid that it might be a mirage, but the more I thought about Alice's invitation, the better an idea it seemed. I set about finding where she was booked to sing and Sid and I went along. Again there was music, laugher and fun. Afterwards, as we all had a drink together, I was pleased to find that the natural high I'd felt through a sense of true friendship hadn't been imagined.

At the end of the evening, Ivy and her husband, Harold, invited us to go along with them to another of Alice's concerts, and before long our nights out had become a regular thing.

Sadly, while my life was picking up, it was becoming obvious to those friends and relations who saw my mother regularly that her health was deteriorating and she could no longer cope with looking after me. The local St Dunstan's Welfare Officer, who knew the situation, went to see mother and Alice, suggesting that Alice take me in as a paying guest. 'If you don't take him,' Ivy said to Alice, 'then I will.' Mother was relieved to be free of the burden and Alice, bless her, was willing to take me on.

Alice was legally separated and had an 11-year-old son, Bobby, who was living with her. My lack of sight and hands didn't seem to bother Bobby at all. He would jump on my back and start mock fights with me, come swimming with me, make me stay with him while he mowed the lawn and drag me back if I slunk off. At the same time, he had no qualms about taking out my glass eyes, washing them and putting them back in, or helping me to put on the crab's claws or my dress hands. We got on like a house on fire, more like a couple of brothers than a man of 32 and a young boy.

I may have been a paying guest but I was treated like one of the family. Alice was taking me under her wing in the nicest, most unaffected way. She realised the vacuum that the end of my business had left in my life, and the state of nervous depression that this, and living at home, had reduced me to.

'We must find something for him to do,' she told Ivy and, in her energetic, practical way, set about doing so.

'You know, Billy, I've heard how you used to sing when you were in POW camp,' she remarked one day. 'Why don't you come along to my singing teacher and take some lessons?'

'Oh, that was nothing,' I muttered, dismissing it with a laugh. 'I just used to warble away to myself when I was wandering round, to cheer myself up. I can't sing.'

'How do you know you can't?'

'Well,' I said, embarrassed, 'even if I could sing, can you imagine me standing up in public and singing? I'd empty the house.'

Alice didn't press the matter any further, but, after I'd thought about it, it didn't seem such a daft idea. I'd always enjoyed music and was happy to join in when there was a sing-song. If nothing else, it would be something to occupy my mind.

'You know that singing idea you had?' I asked a little while later.

'Hmmm,' said Alice, leaving space for me to expand.

'All right, I'll have a go. But don't blame me if your teacher lets out a yell and covers his ears.'

My first singing lesson didn't go too badly and at the end of it I was given a song to learn at home. The task sounded fine until I realised that it was ten pages of music and words.

'I'll never learn all that lot,' I protested.

'Yes you will,' Alice said, her voice both calm and firm. I was beginning to learn that when Alice Jolly had decided something was to happen, happen it did.

For the next two weeks, Alice went over that blooming song with me a hundred or more times, over and over until I had it fixed in my head. She was a hard taskmaster but, to my surprise, I found I quite enjoyed practising. The mental effort of learning the song and the concentration needed to perform it, even in front of an audience of three in the singing teacher's lounge, gave me exactly the sort of stimulus I had lacked. It never occurred to me that it might lead anywhere. Singing, like running the business, was active, and when I was involved with it everything else was forgotten.

The more I learnt about expression and how to project my voice, the more absorbed in singing I became. Singing was something that I could do, admittedly with help, but then I would always need help with most things. There were a million things I couldn't do, but you don't need eyes or hands to sing.

I started entering singing competitions and one day Alice suggested that we practise a duet together, with the idea of performing at a forthcoming charity concert. As I grew more confident in my singing and Alice and I became an experienced duo, the demand for us to give recitals increased, both locally and further afield. It was the beginning of a partnership in song that was to take me to the stage of the Festival Hall, the Old Vic and television. It brought me friends from many countries and different walks of life, but more than anything it gave me a sense of purpose, of contributing something, however modest, to the needs and joys of others. Alice had certainly succeeded in finding me something useful to do.

There was no denying that Alice's friendship had helped me to turn my life around. Inside we both knew that we loved each other, but it took ten years of living under the same roof for me finally to pop the question. To my delight Alice accepted, with one proviso—I needed Bobby's permission. It had taken me all my courage to ask for Alice's hand, and now it seemed that I was having to do it again. I'm sure that Bobby sensed my nerves and, as always, had the knack of making me laugh at myself, joking, 'What took you so long?'

I was hard-up for an answer. Was it that my newfound happiness with Alice seemed to me such a precious thing, and so complete as it was that I was afraid to disturb it? Was it that, deep down, I still lacked the self-confidence to believe that anyone could really be prepared to put up with me for life? I don't know and it doesn't matter, because we were married on 26 May 1962 and are still married 50 years later.

Alice later confessed that, when we were both youngsters, she'd felt that she wasn't good enough for me. The Griffiths, with their own haulage business and the house my grandfather had built on Whalley Old Road, were thought to be a cut above her family. Bloody daft, I say, but that's how it was in our close-knit, Lancashire mill town before the war. Since then, the tables had been turned all right, and it was my turn to feel that I wasn't good enough for her.

For me, marrying Alice was like a miracle. The no-hoper who had returned from POW camp 17 years before, who had been through a fair number of bouts of desolation and despair, had suddenly found himself with a load of interests and surrounded by a loving family. If I'd had fingers I'd have pinched myself to make sure it wasn't a dream.

Strengthened by my new life and family, I decided to return to the Far East on a trip organised by the Java Far East Prisoner of War Club. Many would think everything that happened there would be best forgotten, and as I set foot on Indonesian soil again I thought the same thing. Why was I doing this? Perhaps it was because this land, more than 7000 miles away, held the last memories I had of sight and touch, even if the last few weeks of those had been horrendous— driving through air raids, dodging machine gun attacks and burning oil tanks, diving into ditches and open drains.

Arriving at Tanjong Park, the harbour where we had dis-embarked all that time ago, the memories came back with a force I wasn't expecting. We retraced the road to Garut, walking along the very same ground on which we had set out to rescue the 200 stranded RAF men just before the capitulation. In my head I could still hear bombs going off all round us and frantic shouting. Yet, within that horror, I could also visualise the countryside with its abundance of flowering trees and shrubs. From others' descriptions, it seemed that much of the island's natural beauty was as I'd remembered. Well, almost. Apparently, most women were now wearing Western dress rather than brightly coloured sarongs, so I decided that was one memory I was happy to keep as it was.

Of all the places I visited on my return, none made such an impression on me as the ex-prisoner of war camp, Tjimahi. I had never seen this place, but I remembered the slopes and turnings that led into the building and along the corridor into my old bed space. As I walked those horribly familiar trails, it was as if the years between had never been. Even knowing I was safe, with Alice's arm firmly tucked in mine, I couldn't be certain that we wouldn't face an abusive Japanese guard at the next turn.

Strangely enough, one of the Japanese officers who had been in charge of us was there that day. He was an old chap now, like all of us who survived had become, and had been chatting happily to one of our party until one happened to mention that we were a group of ex-POWs, at which point he hurriedly made his excuses and fled. Apparently he wasn't keen to renew our acquaintance, but, then again, none of us escaped that situation unscathed. He had denied his humanity and had to live with that, just as we had to live with the suffering he'd inflicted.

At Menteng Pulo Cemetery I laid a wreath of poppies at the foot of the memorial cross. Among the crosses we found one to Captain John Rae Smith. He and I had had a bad bout of dysentery at the same time. He had died and here was I, standing by his grave. I felt sad and humble at the memory of all the loss and suffering, yet deeply grateful for having been given the chance to return. While there was much about my time in Java that I wished I could forget, it was important to remember the love and care of friends and comrades who helped me to survive—those who had died there while I lived, and others, like Colonel Dunlop, Mickey de Jonge and Andrew Crighton, whose friendship I'd had the fortune to renew back home. They were all my ministering angels.

Back at the hotel we found ourselves surrounded by Japanese tourists. Alice knew what an emotional trip this was for me. 'Does the sound of all the chatter upset you?' she enquired gently, as a signal that it would be all right to go back to our room if I wanted to.

'Not a bit,' I replied truthfully, 'As long as they're not armed with bamboo truncheons!'

'It's all right,' Alice laughed, 'they're not carrying anything more lethal than cameras.'

As we laughed, I knew that it was all right. To hear that strange yet familiar tongue again after all these years, in such pleasant, luxurious conditions, only underlined the fact of my being free.

I have had a far fuller, richer life than I would have believed possible in the years immediately after my disablement. I learned long ago that to bemoan the loss of what you can never have only leads to disappointment, frustration and unhappiness. The secret is to make the best of things, and for me that has been meeting old friends and making new ones.

I'd say that a strong constitution and a basically cheerful outlook have been my greatest assets, but without Alice to encourage me, to support me with her enthusiasm, humour, no-nonsense care and her love, my life would have been very different.

In my mind I will always be 21, and Alice, I'm sure, hasn't changed at all from the girl I used to dance with before the war. When I feel her arm in mine, as strange as it may sound coming from someone for whom most people automatically feel sorry, I can honestly say, I am lucky.

Reflection

The Revd Fr Rob Taylerson, Parish Priest at St Teresa of the Child Jesus, Stoke-on-Trent, in the Archdiocese of Birmingham

William (Bill) Griffiths, aged 91, shares with us 70 years of his life. It is a concertina of memories. The calamities of Bill's life, which one might have expected to crush his spirit, were many: the blinding and maiming explosion; three-and-a-half-years as a prisoner of war, with hardship, hunger, sickness, deprivation and cruelty; the wife who left him for another; the permanent limitations of blindness and the 'crab's claw' mechanical hands; the blow of a business failure; his initial life path and expectation of driving lorries, with the freedom of the road, all taken from him.

When first maimed, Bill faced self-pity and a desire to end it all. He came through these inner journeys, not as a powerful victor but with the small inner strength of knowing that he cherished life itself. Time gradually brought new blessings and opportunities, unexpected joys and loves, a gifted singing voice, a duet-singing partner and a family with whom he found love and harmony.

Bill's account shows more thoughts of others than of self: he talks of Colonel Dunlop, Mickey de Jonge, Andrew Crighton, Joe Holland, Uncle Robert, Ethel (and the kid), his mother Agnes and her new husband William, Grandpa, Commodore Dacre, his two brothers, Sid Wilding, Ivy Walk-den, Alice Jolly and her son Bobby, and John Rae Smith. For each of them, we learn their place in Billy's life. Each person is described without Bill's eyesight and yet with a clarity that shows us how he sees them. In his hard knocks there is neither condemnation of others nor bitterness. For the generosity and love of others, there is gratitude and esteem. The lack of eyesight on Bill's part does not detract from the pictures he paints. No one with eyesight could paint clearer word-pictures than Bill paints without eyesight. No one could 'see better' who these people are.

For each of us, the path we see for our life gives meaning to our life. If that path is destroyed, 'who we are' and 'what our purpose in life is' can be destroyed too. Faith and hope take a blow, from which many people never recover. Bill's faith and hope did wonderfully recover and grow, eventually with such power that the good he perceives has become more central in his recollections than the evil. This is very powerful.

'I am lucky,' says Bill, and yet, when I read his account, it is the growing inner strength rather than luck that shines through. From where does this strength come? Is it from within Bill? Is it from the love that he has been shown by others? Is it from a religious faith or divine grace? Perhaps it comes from more than one of these. Reflecting on his words brings a challenge for me to see my own life better—to see goodness as he sees it, to see the past in such a way as to be free from condemnations, to value more deeply friendship, love, the generosity of others and the blessings of each day.

What do you think?

- Bill wanted to die but needed help to do so—help that was not forthcoming. At the age of 91, what do you think he would say to his 21-year-old self?
- In the story, we see very different attitudes to life demonstrated through the actions of Colonel 'Weary' Dunlop

and the Japanese guard who almost bayoneted Bill. How would you describe the differences in the attitude to life that lay behind them?

- Bill faced many problems and setbacks. From where and from whom did Bill get the strength to overcome them and go on to live a happy and fulfilled life?

- Bill's final statement is 'I can honestly say, I am lucky.' Do you think that would be the conclusion of those who did not know him but knew only his circumstances?

- What bearing does Bill's story have on the debate about assisted suicide?

- Bill's story is truly inspirational. What impresses you most?

- It is often said that angels are those sent to help us in our need. Bill's strength grew little by little, and at each setback there was someone to help him. Plot his journey as a ladder or series of steps, noting the situation and the helper.

3

A CHANCE TO CHANGE: JOANNE'S STORY

I like to believe that everyone can make good, that people are better than their worst mistakes and that, whatever has happened, a person can put things right again. But what if the mistake was more than a mistake? What if it was a serious crime? What if it was rape? What then?

It was a question that played on my mind for some time— only it wasn't hypothetical. I had been raped and, five years later, was given the opportunity to sit face to face with my attacker (whom I shall call Darren). To most people, the meeting didn't sound like much of an opportunity. Why would I want, ever again, to set eyes on the man who raped me, let alone talk to him? But, although others found it difficult to understand, I did want to. Doing so would be a chance for me to tell him exactly how he made me feel that day, to tell him how his actions had affected my life and my family, and to tell him how I felt now.

Did I hate him? For a while afterwards you could probably say that I did, but you can't go on living with hate in your heart for ever. Well, I can't, anyway. I'm not a person who feels hatred. That feeling isn't me, or it's not the me I recognise, and it's not the me I want to be. Besides, hating him is not going to change what happened.

I could sit there thinking, 'Oh my good God, why has this person done this to me?' Or I could say, 'God help me to forgive and help him to have a better life.' Everyone can change and everyone deserves a chance to change, don't they? As I saw it, I had a choice: I could either hate him for the rest of my life or I could forgive him.

There are people who have criticised me for the choice I made. How could I forgive what he did? How could any sane person forgive what he did? Perhaps these same people think that I don't understand the full horror of the crime. Perhaps they think those words came easily to me. Or maybe they think that I forgave because I'm a Christian and believe it is what I'm supposed to do.

The truth is, people can be quick to judge, to decide for me what it feels like to be raped or how I should feel about it now. Perhaps it's easier that way. To ask how I feel, you have to see me as a real person, as more than a victim of a terrible crime. Terrible things do happen to real people, and those who survive have to find a way to go on living. I could live in the past, stay in that painful place for ever, or I could try to move on. That was what the meeting was about. It wasn't about making excuses. It wasn't easy. It wasn't about God and what I thought I should do. It was about me as a person, looking at another person and thinking, 'What is the good of hating him for the rest of my life?' Hate doesn't change anything—not for the better, anyway. Yes, he did something terrible, but I can't change what happened to me. As sad as the situation is, I'm still here, I've got to get on with my life and he's got to get on with his. I don't want anyone else to have to go through what I went through. I want him to have the best of his life, so that he doesn't rape anyone else. I chose to forgive because I didn't want his mistake to rule my life. It was tough, but I knew in my heart that it was a better way to live, and I prayed for God to help me in this decision, as I believe he does in all things.

After I was raped, I didn't live; I existed. I didn't know how to continue to live in a world where things like this could happen to me. So, in many ways, I didn't. For months I did nothing. I rarely left the house, and when I did, if anyone got too close to me, I moved. Even a strange man walking past me with a shopping trolley was enough to make me uncomfortable. Suddenly, everything in life was uncertain.

I don't suppose that any victim of crime ever expects it to happen to them. I certainly didn't. Even when I saw my attacker standing at the door seconds before, I didn't realise what was coming next. For me, it was a normal working day. It was lunch time. Darren appeared at the door. I recognised him, although I didn't know him well—I knew his name. He asked me a question about what I was doing, then he lunged for me.

Nobody else was in the building at the time, and I felt sure that he wouldn't walk out of there leaving me alive. When he did, I scrambled to the Ladies, locked myself in and called the police.

I was still hiding in a toilet cubicle when the police arrived. A policeman informed my husband that I'd been attacked. He didn't realise it was rape and was traumatised when he found out the full details. I couldn't see him straight away. First I had to go to a medical centre for tests and then on to the police station to be interviewed.

By the time the investigations were finished, it was 10.30 at night. I was pleased to get home so that I could shower, and I stood, for what seemed like ages, letting the water wash over and over me. I wanted to wash myself clean of what had happened, for the water to run off me and take my pain with it. It didn't. However hard I scrubbed, I could still smell him for weeks afterwards, and the cuts and bruises on my body were a visible reminder of what he'd done to me.

Darren was caught that same night. At first he denied the charges, and I worried that I might have to go through the ordeal of a trial. Thankfully, that changed once he was presented with the DNA evidence. His guilty plea meant that I didn't need to go to court. I was glad not to be called to give evidence at a trial, but I still wanted to go to the court for Darren's sentencing because I thought that it would be the only opportunity I'd get to face him. I wanted him to know that I could face him, to prove that I was a survivor and not a victim. I wasn't going to be destroyed by this. I didn't want what he'd done to affect my life any longer. I was going to carry on, and when he saw me standing there, looking strong, he'd see that.

Unfortunately, the court case didn't boost my confidence in the way I'd hoped. I never met my barrister or spoke to anyone who was going to put my point forward in court. Then the judge made a final comment that I couldn't get out of my mind: he told Darren that he had ruined my life. Although I understood why the judge said it, I didn't want Darren to go through life thinking that. I didn't want him to think that what he did to me gave him that kind of power or control over my life.

Of course, at the time, Darren did still have some power

over me—not physically, but in so far as my life was now ruled by fear. I was a 32-year-old married woman, yet inside I was a scared child. All I wanted was for my dad to hold me and tell me that everything would be all right. When I was in his arms, I felt safe, but it was the only place where I did.

It was almost a year after I was raped that a victim liaison officer mentioned restorative justice. I'd never heard of it, but she explained that it was a chance for victims to meet with those responsible for the harm. It was an opportunity for me to meet with Darren in a safe environment where he couldn't hurt me any more. It would be a time when I could hold him accountable for what he'd done, to help him understand the full impact of his actions that day. It sounded like something that I might like to do at some point, even though I didn't feel ready for it at the time.

In my mind I could still hear the judge summing up the case—'You have ruined this woman's life'—and I was determined to show Darren that he hadn't. I was still here. I had survived what he put me through and my happiness didn't belong to him. That wasn't to belittle the impact of the crime or to pretend that it was OK. Of course it wasn't OK. For a time, Darren had indeed destroyed my life and the lives of my family too, and I wanted to tell him exactly the depth of pain he had caused, and not just to me. I wasn't the only one hurt that day. After it happened, my husband kept saying over and over, 'I should have been able to protect you. I'm your husband, I should have been able to protect you.' He was heartbroken that he couldn't. Neither could my mum, dad or brother, but that didn't stop the irrational guilt that haunted them. They all felt pain in different ways and were all suffering because of what Darren did.

I'd been told several times that Darren was doing victim empathy work to help him understand the wider implications of his crime. It seemed odd that someone could be telling him about how his crime had affected me and my family, when no one had asked me. How could anyone else know how I felt that day? Only I knew that.

So one day I asked, 'What is this victim empathy work he's doing?'

'We'll say, "How do you think the victim feels?"' the victim liaison officer told me.

'The victim? Are you calling me by name? Are you saying, "How does Jo feel?"'

'No, we say, "How do you think the victim feels?"'

'Well, how can it be victim empathy, when it's not about me? Unless you've been raped, how can you tell him what that feels like? How can anyone tell him how he made me feel, how he made my family feel?'

It was then that I decided to take up the offer for restorative justice. It was three years after I'd first heard about the programme and I felt ready to do it, to face Darren and tell him exactly how I felt. Not how some anonymous, faceless victim felt, but how a real person, a living human being, felt—how I, Joanne Nodding, felt.

My request was knocked back. I was told that restorative justice wasn't something they did for serious crimes, for crimes like rape. I couldn't believe it. I didn't understand why restorative justice had been mentioned to me in the first place if it wasn't something I could do.

'I'm not letting this stop here,' I said. 'I want to meet him.'

It was clear that I wasn't going to get any further that day. The authorities weren't going to agree, but I was determined to persuade them. I wanted to meet Darren. How else could he understand what he'd done?

My persistence paid off and I was eventually granted funding for the restorative justice programme. At first my family couldn't understand why I wanted to face the man who had raped me. What good could it do? Had I not been hurt by him enough? I could see where they were coming from: they just wanted to protect me. Had I been them, I might have thought the same. In my view, he was locked up, so what harm could he do me now?

At the start of the process, two professionals who were working with Darren visited me to find out more about why I wanted us to meet.

'I'm not angry with him,' I told them honestly. 'He's done it, he's locked up, he's been punished. I'm not trying to punish him any more, but he needs to know what he's done to me and my family. It's all right him going to prison, but however much victim empathy work he is doing, how can he know what he put me and my family through? I am the only one who can tell him that. No one else can because no one else knows.

'I want to get across to him what he's done, because unless he realises how bad it is, he might do it again. He's already done it to me. I'd rather forgive him and let him move on than let him do it to someone else.'

I meant what I said. When I'd first started to think about the meeting, it was about me facing Darren and showing him that what the judge had said that day about him ruining my life wasn't true. I went over and over it all in my head, thinking about what I'd say to him if I had the chance. I could say, 'Darren, I absolutely hate you,' but that wasn't going to change what had happened. Then I started to think about forgiveness—how people can forgive and people do forgive; how I could forgive. But what would that mean?

I didn't have all the answers figured out, but my two visitors seemed satisfied with the reasons I gave. Of course, that wasn't the end of it. Darren still had a say, and if he didn't agree to meet me, then the meeting wouldn't go ahead. It was the third visit before I found out his decision. The support workers came in and started talking, but there was only one thing I wanted them to tell me.

'Is he going to meet me? Has he agreed?' I asked.

'Yes, he has.'

For the first time since starting the restorative justice process, I broke down and cried.

The meeting didn't happen straight away. I had eight months to think about exactly what I was going to say. I was told not to hope for specific answers because I might be disappointed. As it was, I didn't have any expectations of Darren. He'd done what he'd done. I knew what I wanted to say, but I couldn't control how he reacted to it.

I didn't know what Darren was going to say to me and he didn't know what I was going to say to him, but it was a condition of the meeting that the facilitators knew what we were going to say to each other. They had to know what was going to be said because they didn't want more harm to come to me or any harm to come to him.

When the day of the meeting finally arrived, I wasn't nervous. There had been so much preparation, and I'd imagined the day and how it might pan out so many times, that I felt ready to face Darren for real. I knew that he wouldn't be allowed to shout and scream at me. If he did, they would stop the meeting. What could he do to me now? My biggest worry was that he wouldn't turn up.

A friend agreed to come with me. The centre was halfway across the country and it took us just over four hours to drive there, which meant leaving home at 5am for a 9.30am start. On the way, I went over and over what I was going to say in my head.

'I want eye contact with him,' I told my friend.

'It's really hard to have eye contact with someone,' she said realistically.

'Well, I want eye contact with him. I want to look at his face.'

When we got to the building, I was shown the room where the meeting was going to take place. After all the preparation, it suddenly felt very real. I was asked how I wanted the seating arranged. There were two settees in the room and I moved them opposite each other. That way, we would need to face each other and I could look him in the eyes. I also asked for him to be in the room first. I knew that I could walk in and face Darren, but what about him? I didn't want him to walk towards the room and think, 'Oh my God, it's Jo, I can't walk in there.' Then, when it was all set up, I was taken to another room and waited.

'Jo, are you ready?'

I stood up and put my arms around my friend. This was it. My heart beat faster. I was going to meet my rapist. He had agreed to be there. He wasn't forced to be in that room. He had decided that he was going to be there and I appreciated him being there. By just being there, in my mind he was saying to me, 'Jo, I'm going to face you. I'm going to face what I have done.'

As had been agreed, he was already sitting down when I walked into the room. I recognised him, but he didn't look the way I'd remembered. He looked older and his shoulders were rounded, closing in his body defensively. When I sat down, we had eye contact immediately. I later found out that he had asked for eye contact with me too. He wanted to be able to look at me, and he did.

His step-mum was with him, my friend was with me, and there were two mediators. One of the mediators started the meeting by going over the ground rules—things like, if we wanted a break, then we accepted each other having a break, and if we wanted to stop the meeting, we could. Then the mediator handed over to me. 'This is your meeting, Jo. You begin.'

I looked at Darren. His eyes looked scared. What a role reversal. I had been the one terrified that day and now he was afraid of what I might say.

'Thank you very much for agreeing to do this,' I said, 'because if you hadn't agreed, I wouldn't have this opportunity now.'

Darren just looked and didn't say anything.

'What did you think when you heard I wanted to meet you?' I asked.

'I thought you were going to come in this room and scream and shout at me.'

'What would that gain? What's the point of me screaming and shouting at you? It's not going to change what you did to me, is it?'

'No. It's not.'

I started to recall the terrible events of that day.

'You raped me, Darren.'

Again he just looked but said nothing.

'You know, Darren, that day you put me through hell. It was absolutely awful what you put me through. I thought you were going to kill me that day. I did. I really thought I was going to die. You were raping me and I thought you were going to kill me.'

As I said that, something moved in him and he started to cry. I don't think that thought had crossed his mind. I don't think he realised he had terrified me to that extent. To him, the rape was just an opportunity. He never considered his family, my family, or how scared he made me feel that day. He didn't have a clue.

'Who else do you think was affected by what you did?'

He said nothing.

'What about my dad?' I offered.

'What do you mean?'

'My mum and dad? My brother? My husband? How do you think they feel about what you did?'

He said nothing as the tears streaked his face.

'Do you need a break?' I asked.

His step-mum looked at me. 'No, he doesn't need a break. He needs to listen to all of this. He needs to listen to what he put you through.'

'So, what about your lot?'

'I wasn't around when it happened,' his step-mum replied.

'Well, what about your dad? How do you think your dad felt when he got a phone call telling him you had raped me?'

'I'd never even thought about that, Jo. I never even thought about my dad getting a phone call.'

'Well, think about it.' I was calm but firm. 'You need to think about your family.'

I knew it was hard for him to listen to, so a couple of times I changed the conversation to what he was doing now and what he was hoping to do once he was released. We even had a laugh together, something that some people have found difficult to understand.

Then he apologised. 'Jo, I'm sorry, and when I say I'm sorry I mean proper sorry, and I promise you that I won't do this again.'

During the preparation work, I'd been asked, 'How would you feel if he said sorry to you?'

I'd answered, 'I'm not doing this for a sorry. If he says sorry, I'll accept it, but that's not my main reason. I'm not seeing him for him to be remorseful, I'm seeing him because I need to do certain things. I need to forgive him. I need to face him for myself.'

I didn't go expecting a sorry, but when I heard it, I believed him. People can say, 'Oh well, he just said it,' but he didn't have to. He didn't have to agree to that meeting; he didn't have to sit opposite me. He didn't have to apologise, but he did, and it felt genuine.

The meeting lasted an hour and a half. At the end, the mediator asked, 'Have you got anything else to say, Jo?'

I did. I knew that I was going to forgive Darren. I'd done all the preparation work but, when the time came, I had to look away and blink back the tears. It's hard to say you forgive someone who has done that to you, but I needed to do it. I needed to end it here.

'Yes, I've got one thing to say.' I looked at Darren. 'What I'm going to say to you is really, really hard for a lot of people to understand, but I forgive you for what you've done to me, and if you haven't forgiven yourself I want you to forgive yourself. I want you to go on and have a successful life. Hating just eats you up. It doesn't change anything.'

Darren started to cry again. I don't think he could believe what I was saying to him, but as I sat opposite him I felt no hatred. I wanted to let him see good, to let him make good. I wanted him to grow old and have a good life.

His step-mum was wonderful. She didn't try to make any excuses for what he had done. 'Thank you, Jo,' she said as I stood up to leave.

I looked at her as I replied, 'My pleasure.' I meant it.

I had a smile on my face as I walked out. I left feeling fantastic, as if a huge burden had been lifted from me. I'd faced him. I'd looked at him. I'd told him what I needed to. Now he knows how he made me feel. He knows that he put me through a traumatic time. Maybe it will stop him doing it again. Maybe it will help him think about other people in life, and to think about what he wants for his own future.

Now, I could think about my future. I'll never forget that day, but, thanks to the restorative justice programme, I can put it in a drawer and close it. Forgiving Darren gave me my life back and it felt brilliant.

Reflection
Sean Murphy QC

It has been said that rape is a crime which is worse than murder, because the victim has to carry the experience with her every day for the rest of her life. It affects all those who are close to her. That consideration makes Joanne's story all the more remarkable: 'After I was raped, I didn't live; I existed.' Only in her father's arms did she feel safe in any way.

During my career at the Bar, I encountered a number of men who were convicted of rape. On only a few occasions was any significant degree of remorse displayed. Nevertheless, even the worst offender is someone's son or brother or uncle, and his lawyer may be the only person in the world who is still speaking to him.

As a prosecutor, I often met complainers (victims) after trial to answer any questions they might have and to seek to explain what had happened in court: in my jurisdiction (Scotland) that is normal practice nowadays, unlike Joanne's experience elsewhere. Their responses are taken into account when the training programmes for senior prosecutors are under revision. Psychiatric advice indicates that the knowledge that this contribution is valued is itself therapeutic for complainers.

In my experience, the feelings described by Joanne, that her assailant must not be allowed to win in any sense by being allowed to get away with ruining her life, are almost universal in women who have had the courage to come forward to speak of what has happened to them. In many cases, such feelings are a barrier to forgiveness. Joanne, however, has such a capacity for living that she was able to see beyond that barrier and to realise that there was something worth reaching for on the other side.

As Christians, we are taught that we should seek reconciliation with those who have offended us and that this is a reflection of God's love for us: 'Forgive us our trespasses as we forgive those who trespass against us...' It is easy to recite these phrases daily without appreciating how profound their meaning is. When we can bring ourselves to forgive someone who has offended us in a really serious way, we are truly reflecting in the world God's love for us and his forgiveness of us.

The path of reconciliation begins with a single step. Through prayer and in responding to a need within her as a person, Joanne took that step. The process was lengthy and slow before the meeting took place between victim and rapist, between Joanne and Darren. As she says, Joanne is more than a label or a statistic: she is a human being who deserves to live beyond the shadow of the appalling crime that was forced upon her. But Darren, too, is more than a label or statistic: he is also a human being. He has committed an appalling crime but he remains someone valued by God. In her generosity of spirit, Joanne sees the humanity within the man who has raped her. She, the victim, recognises a potential for good in him, which would never feature in any other analysis of the case. Realising that she herself is more than a victim, she becomes able to see that he is more than a rapist. She has the strongest right to condemn him, but she has instead become the strongest advocate of his reconciliation with normal life, with all of us.

Archbishop Oscar Romero once said this:

Christianity is not a collection of truths that one has to believe, of laws one has to keep, a list of prohibitions. That would be repugnant. Christianity is a person that loved me so much that he demands my love. Christianity is Christ.[2]

By reflecting his love and capacity to forgive in her own life, Joanne understands that Christianity is Christ. Do we?

What do you think?

- Joanne demonstrates a very generous spirit when she says, 'I like to believe that people are better than their worst mistakes.' In your experience, is her attitude true of many people?
- Joanne felt that she could not live with hatred in her heart. What are the negative effects of hatred and the positive effects of forgiveness?
- What do you find impressive and special in this account?
- Darren's attack on Joanne was a serious and violent one. What effect do you think this had on her husband and her family?
- Why do you think that the authorities were initially reluctant to allow Joanne to take part in the restorative justice programme?
- In what ways did Joanne's preparation for the meeting work towards a good outcome?
- What do you think Joanne means when she says, 'Forgiving Darren gave me my life back'?

4

TWENTY MINUTES: PENNY'S STORY

At 11.17 am on 15 June 1996, the largest peace-time bomb ever detonated in Great Britain exploded on Corporation Street in Manchester city centre, just yards from where I'd stood 20 minutes earlier. It was a miracle that no one was killed, but lives were changed that day and mine was one of them.

More than 15 years later, I still remember that morning clearly. It was a Saturday and the city was buzzing with Fathers' Day shoppers and thousands of Russians who were in town for the Euro 96 football championships. For me, apart from having to beat my way through extra crowds, it was a working day like any other. As usual, my mind was busying itself with thoughts such as, 'Have we got enough change in the till?' The answer was invariably 'No', and that morning I made two trips to raid other retailers' supplies by paying for Polo mints with £10 notes.

At that time our bookshop, St Denys, was in the Corn Exchange building, just off the street where the bomb exploded. Historically, as the name suggests, it was a place where farmers and merchants traded cereal grains. When we were there, the ground-floor trading hall was a lively market of small stallholders. Above them was a tall atrium covered by a glass dome, through which natural light shone into the middle of the building. We were in a unit on the second floor, facing into the centre. There were no outside windows, so you could say that, once inside, we really were in a world of our own.

When I say 'we', I'm talking about my business partner and friend, Sue. We've been together since the start, and in many ways this story is as much hers as it is mine.

'That's no place for a shop,' people had warned us when we told them of our initial plans. 'No one will ever find you.' Those who were sceptical did have a point. We weren't the type of shop that you would stumble upon. Depending on which entrance you came in at, you could go up two flights of stairs to a mezzanine level and walk a full circle without seeing us. There was a lift of sorts, but it was temperamental, and often customers were left stranded between floors. Luckily it wasn't enclosed so people didn't really mind. At least, they didn't complain. They'd just yell, 'The lift's stuck!' and we'd have to shout down the atrium for someone to shut the cage doors properly and get it going again. As if that wasn't enough of an obstacle to our trade, at weekends we were the only unit open on the upper level, which meant there was the added inconvenience that we and all our customers had to sign in and out.

Still, despite the obstacles, people who wanted to find us succeeded, and over 14 years we had built up a community of regulars, with many friendships made while customers drank our welcome coffee. Once people found us, they tended to come back, and as we were a specialist retailer, they would often travel some distance to shop with us.

On the morning of the bomb, Christopher, a regular customer from across the Pennines, had been browsing for a while when his wife, Joni, burst in. 'There you are,' she said, with a tone expressing both agitation and relief. 'We need to go now.'

'OK. I'll just pay for these,' he said, seemingly unconcerned by her dramatic appearance.

'Well, hurry up,' Joni insisted. 'They're closing the road where the car is. If we don't go now, we'll not get home.'

As Christopher paid, I asked, 'Is everything OK?'

'Sorry about this,' said Joni. 'We've got to rush because our car is parked near the Town Hall. They're evacuating the square mile between Albert Square and Victoria Station. If we don't get it now, I don't know how long we might be stuck.'

It was only after they had left that I suddenly thought, 'That's strange. We're in the square mile between Albert Square and Victoria Station. Why has no one told us to leave?' I walked out of the shop and looked over the banister. By this time on a Saturday, the market hall would usually be bustling with shoppers. Instead it was deserted. My eyes scanned the floor but I couldn't see anyone. Then I spotted a single figure and he was preparing to lock the doors.

'What's going on?' I shouted.

The man looked up. 'What are you doing up there? The building has been evacuated.'

'Well, it would've been nice if someone had told us,' I started.

'Listen, lady, it's no time for arguing. Just get out as quick as you can.'

I didn't understand what was going on. I still had customers and staff in the shop, and what did he mean: 'What are you doing there?' We'd all signed into the building, as we always did on a Saturday, so the security staff knew exactly where we were.

Trying to remain calm and polite, I asked people to leave, but my officious voice obviously wasn't as authoritative as I'd intended because some customers didn't even look up from their books.

The staff were more concerned. 'What's going on, Penny?' they asked.

'The building has been evacuated,' I said, feeling as puzzled about the whole thing as they clearly were. 'Can you help me clear the shop?'

It wasn't as easy as it sounds. We had started the business in two small rooms, but over the years the shop had expanded into the units at either side. We didn't have a tannoy system and, although it probably only took a minute or two to get round all of the customers, it felt like an age. 'I've got to ask you to leave now, I'm sorry,' I repeated, trying to come across as serious but not panicked. 'I'm not allowed to serve any more. I've been told I've got to close now. I'm really sorry, can you leave? Now. Please?'

Certain that everyone was out of the shop, I closed the door behind me, purposefully not locking it. We'd been evacuated six months earlier because of a bomb scare and the police had smashed the door down to search the premises. I was conscious that I didn't want it to happen again. Tidying the mess and getting the door replaced had been a real nuisance.

However, once downstairs, I sensed that this wasn't quite the same as the other scares. 'You can't go out that door,' a fireman told me as I made towards the exit I always used. 'I'm amazed anyone is still in here,' he said, emphasising our need for speed. 'Just get out. Get out as quick as you can.'

Outside, police were cordoning off the building.

'What do you want us to do, Penny?' the staff asked.

I looked around. The city was so quiet—an eerie rather than a peaceful silence.

'Whatever it is, it looks serious,' I said. 'There's no point hanging around here. Just get off home and I'll see you on Monday.'

As I said it, the workaholic in me wondered if I should grab a coffee somewhere and wait to see what was going on. I looked at my watch; it was just before 11 am. We always closed at 1 pm on a Saturday, so, with only a couple of hours of trading left, I decided to call it a day. There was a train on the platform when I got to the station. I jumped on and it pulled away at 11.05 am. Safely on the train, it would be an hour and a half before I knew anything had happened.

Sue wasn't working that morning, but, when either one of us wasn't in the shop, we'd always speak on the phone to check that everything was OK. When she called and there was no answer, she started to get concerned. Her sister, who was working for us that day, rang to let Sue know that we'd had to close the shop. However, as the news of the bomb emerged, Sue's sister could only tell her that we'd got out of the building safely. I'd last been seen heading towards Victoria Station—which had been wrecked in the blast too.

When I arrived home, my husband was beside himself with worry. In today's multimedia world it's hard to imagine not being able to contact someone instantly. Of course there were mobile phones, but many people didn't have one, and I certainly didn't. It was difficult to take in what I was hearing. I'd been there and seen the police cordons. Perhaps I should've been prepared for something like this to happen. The threat of terrorism wasn't anything new. I'd once answered the phone to hear, 'There's a bomb, pass it on.' In my mind I saw a cartoon bomb: we were all passing it along nervously while the wick sizzled. I called the police and was asked to repeat exactly what had been said. Apparently the policeman was listening for code words and, luckily, I didn't have them. Kicking the shop door down, or however they broke it, to search our premises seemed a step up from a hoax call. Yet, although each threat brought with it a wave of anxiety, I never imagined the threat would be carried out for real. I certainly hadn't expected anything like this. Of course I knew these kinds of things happened, but it always happened somewhere else, to someone else. Things like this didn't happen to me.

On the TV news, the cameras kept fixing upon a red pillar box, standing untouched among the dust and rubble. You can still find it there today, with a brass plate commemorating the day it stood tall, protecting its post, while everything crumbled around it. To be honest, I got fed up of seeing it. I felt like shouting at the TV, 'OK, OK, I get that the postbox is all right, but what about the rest of the city?' What I really wanted to know was, what about the Corn Exchange? Part of me held on to the hope that, since it hadn't been mentioned, maybe it wasn't damaged. At the same time, I knew that the blast was so close that the building and our shop couldn't have escaped.

Twenty minutes. The thought hung there like someone whispering repeatedly into my ear. Twenty minutes earlier and I would have been there when the bomb exploded. If I had left the shop 20 minutes later, I wouldn't be here.

I couldn't sleep. I knew I must have walked past the van that was holding the explosives at least twice that morning. Of course I didn't tell anyone I'd been there. I just hoped no one would tell the police that they'd seen a skinny girl in a hood in the vicinity of the bomb. If they did, what could I say? I hadn't seen anything. I'm not very observant at the best of times. All I was thinking about was making sure I had enough change in the till. I must have walked past it—the van that held a bomb that blew up the city I called home, and destroyed my livelihood with it. I replayed the morning's events over and over in my head, but nothing. I had stood right next to the van carrying the bomb, and hadn't even noticed it was there.

I kept watching the clock. Twenty minutes I spent in the shower; I was on the phone for 20 minutes; 20 minutes went by while I drank a cup of coffee. Twenty minutes. In the shop, 20 minutes would go by in such a flash, it was frightening to think how, in a world of sliding doors, 20 minutes had made such a difference to my life. That morning, although I hadn't known it, 20 minutes was all the time I had. For me it could so easily have been all the time in the world.

No matter how much I heard about the blast on the radio and TV, the day's events still didn't seem real to me. I needed to see what had happened for myself, to see our shop and to know that everything was going to be all right. The next morning my husband drove me into the city, but as we got nearer to the centre it was clear that we weren't going to find the reassurance I'd been hoping for. We drove for miles around the outskirts, trying to find a route in, but all the roads had been closed. Eventually we gave up, parked about a mile away from the city centre and walked.

We didn't need to get close to realise that this wasn't the same city that I'd left the day before. The air was heavy with dust and you couldn't hear yourself speak for the sound of alarms—dozens and dozens of alarms—as if the buildings themselves were crying out in distress.

Along Deansgate, usually one of the busiest streets through the city centre, shop windows, or what was left of the windows, were being boarded up. I don't think that any stores were open for business—not that many people would have felt like shopping, even if they were.

Even on foot we couldn't get anywhere near the Corn Exchange. Someone told us that people were meeting at the Town Hall, where we might be able to find out more information. We didn't.

For days we returned to the Town Hall. Each day we'd wait, and each day we'd go home hoping that tomorrow would bring more news. Frustratingly, there never seemed to be a tomorrow when we did know more. Our business was going down the pan and there was nothing we could do to stop it. Neither could I stop that nagging thought: 20 minutes and we would've all been dead.

As it was, we were still here. There was that to be thankful for, but it was hard to feel thankful. Everything was gone; we didn't even have the names and addresses of suppliers and customers to let them know what had happened. Where did we go now? How could we move on from this? Everything had gone, and not because I'd done something wrong or failed to do something, like pay a bill or lock the door. Nothing I could have done, and nothing I could ever do, was going to get it back.

It was hard to comprehend how our business had survived so many setbacks over the years for such a random act of violence to destroy it. When we started out, no one had expected us to succeed, and not simply because we'd chosen an out-of-the way location. The country was in recession and it was a difficult time for any business. Indeed, losing my job had been the incentive for us to go it alone.

My vision was always that I would be an archaeologist. That was the subject I studied at Durham University, and it was a huge disappointment to find that, after all my hard work, once I graduated there was no job for me. There was archaeological work that I could have done, but it was all voluntary work and, after years of being a student, I needed to start earning. Finding a paid job, however, was proving impossible. It was no longer a case of what I wanted to do but what I could do, so when my vicar mentioned the chance of work in a bookshop, I jumped at it.

It was there that I met Sue. She had been working at the same shop for four or five years, which seemed very established, even though she was only 21 at the time. We hit it off immediately, so much so that it almost didn't feel like work. It was fun, as if we were playing shops, and, although I wasn't digging around in the earth, as I'd always dreamed I would be, I was really enjoying myself.

I wondered if this could be my real job—what I did as a grown-up, as it were. I loved books and I also enjoyed retail. As a teenager I'd had a Saturday job in a shop and had always been happy to go into work. Life in the shop was never dull. The contact with different people meant that the time passed quickly, chatting to customers was interesting, and I liked the challenge of selling things.

Books and retail were passions I'd had from being a girl, but I had never really thought about them, especially not in terms of a job, until now. However, no sooner had I changed the image of my future from archaeologist to bookseller than everything changed again.

I'd barely got started in the world of work when I was made redundant. I hadn't had a chance to show what I could do. Looking back, it was a simple case of last in, first out, but at the time I saw it as a rejection of me, and it hurt. I was bemoaning my situation when an acquaintance remarked, 'Why don't you open your own bookshop?'

I don't know if it was the naivety of youth or being so fired up from a need to prove myself, but I thought, 'Do you know what? That is exactly what I'll do. I'll set up an academic bookshop selling theological books.' I smile now, thinking about how serious I must have sounded, but then again I *was* serious, because, more than anything, I wanted to be taken seriously.

I stomped around Manchester looking for suitable premises, and Sue, who had been hurt by my redundancy debacle too, joined me in her lunch hour.

The recession, although it was the cause of my being unemployed, served in our favour because businesses were closing faster than others could replace them, leaving a lot of empty units for us to view. At the time, the Conservative government under Margaret Thatcher decided to offer start-up loans for small businesses. It meant that, for a higher rate of interest, we could get an unsecured loan, which the government guaranteed. If anything went wrong, the bank was safe and, more importantly for us setting up, so were we.

Starting off in business felt like an awesome task, but it

wasn't the struggle that we'd initially thought it might be. Inspirational people appeared to help and advise us at every step. We were so busy with the rush of it all that we didn't recognise just how amazing our being in the right place at the right time was.

The first bank manager we met was a woman, who thought it was just wonderful that two young women wanted to set up a business. She agreed an £8000 loan and put us in touch with one of her staff, a Salvation Army man, who helped us to write a business plan. Both were convinced that we were going to succeed and their enthusiasm fuelled ours, providing much-needed energy to get the business off the ground.

Everything we had went into the shop. We worked long hours and took very little out in terms of wages. Although we knew that the loan was safe, we were keen to pay it back as soon as we could. If we could save by doing extra work, then we did, even when that meant sitting up half the night making our own palm crosses for Palm Sunday services—all 60,000 of them! For years we did that, but, while it was really hard on the hands, there were benefits. As I soon discovered, plaiting crosses was always a good way to get a seat to myself on the bus. After all, who wants to sit next to the religious freak?

I didn't care what people thought of me, though. My mind was on a single track. If it was good for business, then it was good for me. Saying that, I did think it a step too far when someone asked me to transport a large wooden crucifix from Goldthorpe in Barnsley to Manchester. 'I'm not bringing a six-foot crucifix on the train. It's just not happening,' I insisted. However, my resistance didn't last long. Three days later I threw a bin bag over it and found myself sitting in a rail carriage, propping up the crucifix I'd sworn I wouldn't carry. That was life.

Together, Sue and I were following a dream. If we weren't in the shop, we were trying to tell people about it, racing around in Sue's battered old Rascal van, attending as many Christian events as we could, like church groupies. Perhaps it wasn't surprising that we later both found ourselves married to clergymen.

Although hard work, it never felt that way, and it wasn't long before our determination to deliver the best possible service began to pay off. In the 1980s, the book trade wasn't like it is today. Now you can order almost anything you like over the internet, but back then there was a real challenge in tracking down an unusual title, and, always up for a challenge, we soon developed a reputation for being able to get hold of any book.

I'd often be jumping on buses and dashing across town to deliver books. When I turned up in person to ensure that the principal of one of Manchester's theological colleges received his book order before 5 pm, he seemed both impressed and intrigued, duly setting me a task to hunt down a copy of a rare Scandinavian text.

'If you can get this book for me, then you can have our library order,' he challenged me.

I still don't know how we did it, because it felt like a fluke when the book arrived within a few days. The principal was impressed and, true to his word, placed the order for the college library with our shop.

Having such a big order really helped to keep us going in those early days. We were always too busy to think very much about what we had achieved, so we were stunned when, 18 months later, the bank manager told us, 'Out of 200 companies who took out those government start-up loans, only five are still in business.' We were one of the five.

I thought about that as I stood looking at the ruins of our business. We'd been fighters then. Sometimes it seemed that they, the faceless bombers, whoever they were, had not just stolen our business; they'd stolen our fight from us, too.

I didn't even have the fight to be angry. More than anything, I was hurt. I didn't give much thought to the bombers. They'd done what they'd done and now we were all paying for it. But what about the people who knew us? What about the security staff? Were we so invisible? Why did nobody come for us? Why, when everyone else had been evacuated from the building, did nobody care that we were still in there?

Usually security made such a fuss about people coming into the building on a Saturday. Why had nobody checked the list to see who had signed in that day and not signed out again? I felt we'd been forgotten because we didn't matter enough. No one cared whether I had been in the Corn Exchange or not, so why would anyone care that all my life's work, everything I'd ever done, had been destroyed in an instant? If no one else cared, then why should I?

It felt as if all I ever did was sit in the Town Hall, waiting for information that never came. It was hard to know what to think. One minute I'd feel helpless, believing, 'I can't do this any more. I want to go home; it's not worth it.' The next I'd be defiant, vowing, 'I haven't got to this point to let them beat me.' By 'they', I didn't mean anyone in particular. I didn't know who had pushed me to the ground and I didn't care. All I wanted was a hand to help me up again, to not stay down and be beaten.

I still held out hope that once we were able to get back inside the building, things would get easier—but they didn't. Seeing the damage just brought me face to face with a different reality. I could fool myself no longer. There was no hope that this situation would resolve itself easily. It wasn't OK, and, worse than that, I couldn't see a way that it could ever be OK again.

Inside the building, the stench was overwhelming. I'd always known that bombs were made of manure, but it had never occurred to me that the smell would be so pungent. There was glass everywhere and it was hard to see where to step without treading on it. I looked up and saw the chair I'd been sitting on, the morning of the explosion. It was lodged in the window, upside down, half in and half out, the back holding it in with the legs in the air. I couldn't help thinking, 'What if Joni hadn't come for her husband?' I would have been catapulted through the window and into the middle of the Corn Exchange. This was the reality of my '20 minutes' nightmare. My stomach turned over at the thought of it and, no matter how many times I told myself that I *hadn't* been sitting on that chair as it was hurled through the air, the image was in my head and I couldn't shake it.

It all seemed so unfair. I shouldn't be here looking at this. I was supposed to be looking forward to my holiday. I was supposed to be going to Canada with my family for three weeks. It had been booked for months, but how could I go and enjoy it now? How could I go when there was so much uncertainty? Sue persuaded me that it would do me good to get away, but I wasn't so sure. I couldn't see how anything would do any good any more, but I knew that it would be unfair on my family to cancel, so I went.

Although the break didn't magically make all my problems disappear, it did give me some renewed strength with which to handle them. While I was away, Sue rescued our files so that we could start contacting customers and suppliers, and, as a stop-gap, Manchester Cathedral allowed us to set up shop in its Chapter House. Other unexpected help came from a publisher's representative who told us that Lichfield Cathedral had recently had a refit. If we were able to collect the old bookshelves, then they were ours, and Sue wasted no time in driving our faithful old van to pick them up. At the same time, some publishers, on hearing of our situation, sent boxes of books on the basis that we would pay for them when we could.

When I got home, Sue had set everything up, ready for us to start trading again. It was amazing, and something that I'd never have believed possible just three weeks earlier.

Although it was sometimes hard to see how we would get back on our feet again, other people's offers of help and messages of support gave us the confidence to carry on. It was very generous of the Dean to offer us space, because Manchester Cathedral had been damaged in the blast too. At the time, he probably thought that our moving in would only be a for a few weeks, as we all did. However, the Corn Exchange building was condemned shortly afterwards, dashing any hopes we had of moving back. Some weeks later, all the contents of the old shop, including a pot full of mouldy coffee, were sent shooting down huge orange plastic tubes and into crates on the street below.

Our insurers insisted that we go through everything and see what could be salvaged. St Peter's House on Oxford Road kindly allowed us to store the crates in the basement, although, again, I don't think they realised just what they'd let themselves in for. We took up nearly the whole space and, after festering all summer, what was left of the contents of our shop smelt like a farmyard.

Wading through it all was exhausting. I couldn't see the point in cataloguing filthy, greasy books that were full of glass splinters. To me, each one was a personal reminder of what we'd lost, and I didn't want any of them. I didn't want to see any of them ever again. To keep at it, I kept reminding myself that we were lucky to have any terrorism insurance at all. Many other businesses had waived theirs because it was an expensive thing to pay for, especially when, politically, things had been looking up. Two years earlier, the IRA had announced a ceasefire. But then, after about 18 months of peace, the fighting started up again with a bomb in London, which killed two people. The bomb in Manchester was much bigger, and yet, despite there being 80,000 people in the city centre that morning, no one was killed. I had to try to keep that in mind. I also needed to remember that, however hurt I felt, I had been one of the lucky ones. I escaped injury from flying glass and debris. Hundreds didn't. I didn't even hear the bomb or feel the blast. Yet, while I knew all of that and tried to be grateful, I couldn't stop the nightmares that haunted me with the fear of what might have been.

Of course, I'd put on a brave face, telling customers, 'We are not about to let this catastrophe put a stop to our work, and we now intend to start from scratch to rebuild our business.' Yet, I was conscious that in all the mayhem we had let some people down. For now at least, I couldn't promise business as usual. I couldn't even promise to be Penny as usual, because I didn't feel like myself. I was uptight and could lose the plot very quickly.

The insurers were making what I thought were unreasonable demands of us and wouldn't pay out until we started up in our own premises again. In turn, I began to make my own demands of the insurers, adamant that if any of the stock was sold on, it shouldn't be sold for use by children because it might have glass in it. Of course, as much as I liked to think I could influence what was happening, we had little control of it, and some things were sold on—something we only found out because people told us later, 'We got some good bargains from your shop.'

For a while, life felt like a constant battle, with no chance of reclaiming the ground we'd once had. After all the effort of cataloguing the stock, there was still no sign of a cheque from the insurance company. We were running out of options. Our only chance was to queue up at the Town Hall to ask for a loan from the Lord Mayor's emergency fund, the thought of which made me uncomfortable, as if we were begging for money.

We were only one of more than 100 small businesses in and around the immediate area that had been forced to close, but the good news was that we were approved for a loan. At least now we had a chance of starting again.

The destruction had left many businesses looking for new premises. There were some units to let in Victoria Station, which we thought might work, but we were told that, being a spiritual bookshop, we weren't the right sort and wouldn't be attracting the right clientéle for the area. Goodness knows what they thought we were selling or who our customers would be. Had we been a film bookshop, they told us, that might have been different.

Eventually we found a place in Manchester's Northern Quarter. These days, the area is known as the city's fashionable or creative district because of the growth in independent shops and businesses, as well as being home to the occasional Hollywood film crew, attracted by its towering buildings and pre-war architecture. Back in the late 1990s, the area was an unknown quantity and quite derelict, but while we were being shown around the premises, we saw a familiar face go past the window.

'See, our customers live here, so it must be OK,' Sue smiled. Looking for any kind of reassurance, we took it.

We made the best of our new location, but in reality the move brought one problem after another. Before we'd even put up our first shelves, there was a fire in the building next door and it had to be demolished. The rebuilding didn't go smoothly and we ended up with damp down one side of the building and a cellar knee-deep in water.

'Do you think someone is trying to tell us something?' Sue joked.

I looked at her as we both stood there in our wellies, and smiled, 'Well, if they are, we're not listening.'

Another 16 years have passed since then and we have recently moved again. You'll find us now in the basement of Manchester Cathedral's visitors' centre, a stone's throw from the Corn Exchange. Everything here—the stock, the furniture, the shelves—was brought from our old bookshop on Oak Street. We didn't have the money to pay for removals, so we moved everything ourselves, with the help of family and friends. Ordinarily that would have been fine. Unfortunately for us, after we had chosen our moving date, protestors against government cuts decided to march through

Manchester city centre on the same Sunday. Consequently, the road we had planned to drive down was closed and we ended up parking as close as we could, walking with full arms for the final 500 metres.

'I'm 57. I shouldn't be doing this,' I thought, struggling to hold up one end of a wooden bookshelf as we scurried along the pavements in Manchester's infamous rain. I'd never considered age before, or what I 'should' be doing, and once we were in the dry, with the coffee brewing, I was able to laugh about it.

Thirty thousand people took to the streets that day, chanting, 'No ifs, no buts, no Tory cuts!' Very few have been untouched by this global recession. It's not been easy for us, either. The poor economic outlook, coupled with changes to the book market brought about by the rise of the internet, has hit us hard. By moving, we were doing something practical and positive about taking our business into the future. It also felt as if, after 16 years, we were finally coming home. We just weren't quite there yet.

The shop was full of boxes, so many that it was hard to imagine where everything would fit. Sue stood staring at an empty shelf. 'Do you want to make everyone some coffee?' I asked, casually trying to get her attention. She snapped out of her trance and, after a short break, was stuck into the unpacking with the rest of us. Sue later told me, 'It was such an odd feeling. I knew what I should be doing but I couldn't do it. I just saw the piles of boxes and felt so overwhelmed by it all.' I knew how she felt. There were so many memories being dismantled and rebuilt, it was hard not to lose yourself in the past.

These days, you might hear people say that the bomb did

Manchester a favour. Of course, these are people who weren't there to witness the terror of that day. When it happened, none of us felt the hand of good fortune.

Of course, Manchester survived and rebuilt itself—some might say, defiantly—into a towering city of glass. It's odd how people's efforts to make the best of a bad situation can obscure the bad to such an extent that it isn't even viewed as such any longer. The destruction and devastation of that day cannot and should not be seen as a good thing. Looking back, though, aside from all the pain, I see the capacity of the human spirit to make good, however dark a situation may appear.

The memory of the bomb has never left me, but I have learned to live with it without being ruled by its fear. The riots in August 2011 brought back to the surface some of the emotions associated with the bomb, that I thought I'd finally put to bed. I watched the violence unfold on TV, not knowing if our shop would be one of those looted and vandalised. Thankfully it wasn't, but seeing so many windows boarded up triggered a reaction from long ago and the nightmares started again. I realised then that the fear of that day, so long ago now, hadn't gone completely, and I can't say that it ever will. What I do know is that it doesn't take up the same space in my thoughts that it once did, and I have more faith that things will work out, even if I can't see how.

After 30 years, we are more or less back to where it all began. Every day, when I look across the street to the Corn Exchange, I think of the girls we once were. Yet, looking through old files, I'm reminded of just how much things have changed—and how much we have changed. We are more aware of how easily lives can take a different turn in a matter of minutes, but we are also more grateful—grateful to be still in business, for all the help we've had along the way, and for the energy of those early days.

Reading some of the letters we wrote when we started out made me think about how brave and confident we once were. We were so much more sure of ourselves, yet also so naive. I found the letter we wrote to the Dean of Manchester Cathedral, asking if he was happy for us to call ourselves St Denys. Because the Cathedral is the Church of St Mary, St Denys and St George, we thought it would be polite to ask, but the letter was written in the full expectation that he would say 'yes'. There was no reason why he should be helpful, but, in our minds at the time, he was going to say 'yes'. We had no doubt. We were Penny and Sue, and we were opening a bookshop: why wouldn't he want to help us?

The Dean replied that the Cathedral was perfectly happy for us to use the name, but it didn't mean that the Cathedral held any responsibility for us. In hindsight, probably a lot of the elderly hierarchy of the church didn't think we were going to last. It's funny how things turn out. The name St Denys fits in well with the Cathedral now, but when we chose it, who'd have thought that one day that's where we would be, and where we'd find the spark of our old selves in the excitement of a fresh challenge and a new start.

Reflection
The Revd Dr Brian Haymes, Baptist Minister, Manchester

The shocking consequences of terrorist acts across the world are frequently flashed across our TV screens. We see bombs exploding, buildings burning and emergency services in full action, and, although we are aware of the horror unfolding, we often watch with an understandable detachment. We think of these often faceless crimes as something happening somewhere else to somebody else. Yet behind the dramatic pictures are many personal stories, like Penny's, that we never hear, and there are hurts that continue long after the news crews have left.

Reading Penny's (and Sue's) story of disasters and determination, I found myself recalling the old war-time slogan that has recently experienced a new lease of life: 'Keep Calm and Carry On'. Like many slogans, it disguises a depth, in this case, of pain, cost and serious resolution in life. People who appear to be calm in moments of disaster and confusion while others collapse, paralysed by fears resulting in a resigned throwing-in of the towel, often disguise the immense, costly and painful struggles that go on deep below the surface. They carry on, but their nightmares are real and long-lived. It costs them to be the people they are. Their apparent calm indicates inner strength of character. That is why there is an inspirational quality to their lives and stories.

St Denys bookshop was born in struggle and has survived by struggling. Together, Penny and Sue worked through re-cession, redundancy and constant changes to the market in which they were working. However, the bomb was one blow from which they often felt there could be no recovery, leaving a trail of wounds, feelings of being beaten unfairly and treated unjustly.

Their reaction could so easily have become hatred, the kind of hatred aimed at no one in particular but creating a collective enemy, a prejudice born and nurtured by fear. How often do we see such prejudices grow old and fester, leading to further acts of violence? Rather than the healing we long for, seeking revenge leads to continuing bitterness, pain and further carnage, but, as Penny discovered, there is often goodness to be found in the darkest of places. Grace is given. It shows itself in the kind actions of others, signalling the surprising renewing presence of God.

It is obvious that Penny and Sue have been driven by deep convictions about the value of their work. Theirs is a story of determination but also of great friendship. I have known the St Denys bookshop almost from its beginning and, from the first, service has characterised its life. Penny's account gives some indication of the ways in which this found expression, even to carrying a bagged-up six-foot crucifix on a train to meet a promised delivery. Their little van seems to have been in constant motion as they made deliveries all over Greater Manchester. How many conferences were helped by a bookstall serviced by St Denys? How many visits were made to theological colleges and universities so that student and staff needs could be met? Sue and Penny simply put themselves out to serve others. It would be boringly true to point out that there has obviously been an element of self-interest in the work—getting a business up and running and keeping it going—but those who have been at the receiving end have often sensed the commitment of these two women to their task. They believe in its value and worth. They have lived their convictions. It is not only the overcoming of huge setbacks, which sometimes crashed into their hope and labours, that is inspiring. It is the steady, quiet, helpful human service that has been offered.

For Penny and Sue, disasters are met by determined dedication. They carry scars but don't talk about them much. The New Testament has a word for this, a virtue not highly prized in our generation: it is 'endurance'. The letter to the Hebrews underlines the significance of endurance and determination in the face of disaster and unsought opposition. This is the way of faithful discipleship. Others may do wicked things that threaten our livelihoods, our sanity and sometimes our lives. Yet, by focusing on Jesus, our example, the pioneer and perfecter of our faith (Hebrews 12:2), we are able to keep holding on, running the race before us and not giving up.

What do you think?

- Penny and Sue embarked on their business venture in a time of recession and high unemployment. What do you think led to their success at such a difficult time?
- Security failed to inform Penny and Sue of the need to evacuate the premises, leaving Penny with feelings of un-importance and worthlessness. Given the situation, how would you account for this omission? Does this experience resonate with you in any way?
- Penny says, 'Sometimes it seemed that they, the faceless bombers, whoever they were, had not just stolen our business; they'd stolen our fight.' Penny's story is one of many that didn't make the headlines, but the effect on

her life and the lives of others was devastating. Can such acts of terrorism ever be justified?

- After the bombing, Penny had many moments where she couldn't help thinking about what might have happened. These thoughts made her stomach turn and embedded the image of destruction in her brain. What, if anything, can we learn from such 'what if' thoughts?
- What can we learn about the nature of friendship from the way in which Penny and Sue supported each other in their time of stress?
- Although Penny sees the capacity of the human spirit to make good, however dark the situation, she objects to the idea that the bombing was good for Manchester. Are there any dangers in over-emphasising the positives of a disaster such as this one?
- In his reflection, the Revd Brian Haymes says, 'Grace is given. It shows itself in the kind actions of others, signalling the surprising renewing presence of God'. Reading through Penny's account, where do you see the renewing presence of God?

PART 2

Forgiveness in everyday life

Love… keeps no record of wrongs.
1 CORINTHIANS 13:5 (NIV)

5

BLOSSOM WHERE YOU ARE PLANTED: TERRY'S STORY

It's often said that you have to get to the bottom before you can get up again. Well, wherever I was, I knew that I had to get up. I had been on the sick for eight months and had lost three stones in weight. I didn't know what was wrong with me and, more worryingly, neither did my doctor. My mates stopped coming round to visit, or most of them did. I guess they didn't know how to handle it, and who could blame them? I'm sure many thought I was dying or wasting away with AIDs. Like I say, I didn't know what was troubling me and, if I'm honest, I didn't have the strength to care.

'You could have ME,' one doctor eventually suggested. That knowledge didn't help much because, at the time, medics still didn't know much about the condition. As far as I could tell, it was no more than a convenient label for all those seemingly unfathomable conditions of weariness. There was no treatment he could offer me, but there was a support group that he recommend I try. So there I was, in a circle of exhausted souls, waiting until their eyes turned on me to share my story of pain. I wanted to scream, 'No, this isn't me! This person you see sitting here, it isn't me!' Each person had a slightly different tale to tell but, as they spoke, their words became a blur. All I could hear was the length of time that people had felt this way, as if they were wearing their suffering like a badge of honour. If that sounds cruel, at the time I didn't care. I was drowning in self-pity. If this was going to be me for the rest of my life, then, quite frankly, I'd rather be dead.

The truth was, at 32 years old I didn't know who I was any more. The Terry Doyle of the past was a legend on Teesside. He was one of the lads in every sense, renowned for both his physical fitness and his ability to drink anyone under the table. He was a die-hard Boro fan and good football player, too—an accomplished martial artist and a cyclist of stamina, who had ridden from Lands End to John O'Groats without breaking much of a sweat. He had a good job and a loving family. Where was that man now?

OK, maybe I wasn't quite the superman I'm portraying here, but it was true compared to the man I had become— the man who was struggling to sit up straight on a plastic chair; the man who would go home to a bare flat with empty cupboards, stare at the TV, wake up with nowhere to go and try to muster the energy to wash.

My divorce had hit me hard. I was a lad about town when I met my wife. I laboured by day and played in punk bands at night. School had meant nothing to me, but I knew I had a brain. So, after I got married, I thought it was about time that I used it, and I went back to college. Working full-time and studying at night wasn't easy but eventually the hard work paid off when I got my degree and landed a job selling petrochemicals. The irony was, I was never any good at chemistry. I failed my chemistry O Level, yet there I was selling the likes of ethylene glycol and toluene, and doing really well at it. If I had nothing else, I had the gift of the gab. To me it was a game, and one in which I kept winning promotion after promotion.

At first I didn't notice the stress; I just kept climbing up the company ladder. I was always looking to the next rung, but the higher I got, the less fun the job became. You know how sometimes when you climb a ladder you get to the top and realise that the ladder is on the wrong wall? Well, I guess that's what I'd done.

By this time, my wife and I had outgrown each other. Aside from our daughter, there was no common ground between us, but knowing that didn't stop the hurt, the anger, and the guilt that weighed so heavy it was becoming impossible to move. One morning after the split, I was driving to work when the car in front cut me up—deliberately, I'm sure. I hit my horn. The driver turned and gave me the finger; he was laughing. I was enraged. I put my foot down and chased that bloke for an hour and a half. If I'd got hold of him, I would've ripped his head off. He must have sensed that too, because he didn't stop. Eventually I gave up the chase. I stormed into work late and tore off my jacket, sending piles of paper flying off the desk. Everyone looked up, but no one said anything. It was as if I'd let out a big roar, warning everyone and everything to leave me alone.

Shortly after that, I caught chicken pox—a child's disease, or so I thought. I don't know how I'd managed to escape it when I was younger. Apparently it hits you worse, the older you are. It's a contagious disease and I had to stay off work. Months later, the chicken pox was gone but I was still out of the office. I wasn't lost in being busy any more. I didn't have anything to do or anywhere to be. For once, I had time to look at myself and, unfortunately for me, I didn't like what I saw.

I didn't want to be the man I had become, but it was only when I was sitting in the support group, surrounded by other people who appeared trapped in a cycle of pain, that my own hopelessness suddenly became overwhelming. Whoever or whatever I thought I was, I wasn't that any more. I was the man who found it difficult to walk to the end of the street. Even getting to the support group—this meeting of losers, as I saw it—had been an ordeal. I flicked through the leaflet the group leader had given us. I scanned it, but only read doom and gloom. I closed my eyes like a child, pretending, if only for a brief moment, that this wasn't happening to me.

I don't know why I thought that I could look after another living being when it was clear to everyone else that I couldn't even look after myself, but after that meeting I walked into the local dog rescue centre and brought home a little mongrel called Prince. I didn't notice much what he looked like, but things like that didn't bother Prince. Simple things kept that dog happy. As long as he had food, exercise and a pat on the head every now and again, to him he had it all. My erratic moods didn't seem to bother him, either. Whatever I was feeling, he was there, looking into my eyes, wagging his tail, loving me no matter what. Sometimes I'd look at him wagging his tail and think, 'What can you see, boy? Why do you love a pathetic old fool like me?' Even if I told myself that no person in the world loved me, I couldn't deny that dog did. Just having him next to me, relying on me, gave me confidence again. Going outside felt less of an effort with Prince by my side. I felt OK when I was with him. When we were together, I could walk to the end of the street and across the next street, then to the park. I'd done it and nothing bad had happened to me. I started to feel safe again. Perhaps I could begin to try doing other things that had frightened me, too?

The church was one of those skeletons that had raised its head while I'd been sat at home. Except for getting married, I'd scarcely set foot inside a church since I was 15. Yet, despite the time that had passed, I begrudged its influence on my life and blamed the church for the paralysing, guilt-ridden conscience it had left me with. Many of my school teachers had been nuns from the order The Sisters of Mercy, or the Sisters of No Mercy, as we used to call them. On a Monday morning they'd ask us what colour vestment the priest had been wearing at Mass, just to check we had been in attendance. God help the poor kid who hadn't noticed, although we soon learned to pay more attention to the priest's clothes than his prayers.

As I got older, I became an altar boy, but all I could remember about it was being bossed around and feeling afraid. I didn't like wearing a cassock: it felt heavy and cumbersome, particularly in the summer. One summer when I was about 14, I could feel myself getting too hot, but I stood there sweltering until suddenly it became too much. My mouth filled with saliva and I ran for the sacristy, where my breakfast came back up all over the floor. Feeling momentarily relieved, I turned to see that the priest had followed me. I thought he'd realised that I was unwell and was going to offer me a glass of water. Instead he clipped me round the ear, snarling, 'How dare you defile the blessed sacrament?' Perhaps he thought that I was hung over from the night before, but I didn't stick around to explain otherwise. I walked out of the church and, except for my wedding day, I never went back.

Almost 17 years had passed since that incident. I was a boy then and that priest had probably forgotten me long ago. Why was I still bothered? I didn't know, but I wanted to talk to a priest, to tell him what was going on in my life, how I'd rejected the church and its teachings, and about the fear and the hypocrisy that, to me, the church represented. I wanted to tell him all the negative thoughts about the church that were taking up space in my head—stuff and bile that I needed to get out.

When I finally struck up the courage to approach a church and speak my mind, the priest didn't react as I had expected at all. He seemed to welcome me as someone who was worthy of God's love, and it felt different, radically different from what I had left. We talked about life being a blessing and a gift. I was always brought up to believe that I had to earn the love of God. I had to be a good boy, play by the rules and conform. I hadn't done any of that, yet here was this man treating me like the prodigal son, telling me that we are already loved by God and that our journey is to discover that fact. It was a message of unconditional love, which was there for me all the time, if only I would use my free will to choose it. I walked away from the church feeling as if I'd set off on a journey of exploration, to find what had always been there, if only I could see it.

Being ill had humbled me. I no longer believed that I had all the answers or that taking a tablet or downing a few pints would make life better. If medical science couldn't help me, then I needed to discover what could. I didn't feel strong enough to play football or practise martial arts, but I felt sociable enough to try a yoga class. Of course, that was difficult for other reasons. I was a lad from South Bank and we didn't do that kind of stuff. It wasn't a case of getting in touch with my feminine side. When you grow up in South Bank as a man, you're not supposed to have a feminine side, especially not when you're six feet tall and built like I am. As was to be expected, I was the only bloke there. I found a space at the back and, despite feeling stupid, I kept going. I started going to Mass too, and eventually I went back to work as well.

At first I returned to the office part-time. My employer was brilliant, but I knew that my life had changed and there was no going back. Being laid up had given me time to reevaluate what was important to me and my career—or, rather, I realised that the career I had no longer mattered in the same way. I negotiated a voluntary severance and used the money to fund myself through three years of study at the College of Oriental Medicine in Sheffield. I completely reinvented myself and, for a time, it felt good.

I was keen to share what I was learning with the people at my church, the place I had reached out to and found comfort in when I was ill. It didn't go down well. My ideas of introducing traditional Chinese medicine and exercise were looked upon with scepticism. I felt rejected, and all the old feelings I thought I'd resolved rose up again. To me it was the same old hypocritical church that was all about putting your best clothes on for a Sunday morning ritual and then behaving however you liked for the rest of the week. Why had I thought it would be any different? I'd thought times had changed; I'd thought I had changed, that things like this wouldn't bother me as much any more. Perhaps I hadn't changed, not really—not in the way I viewed the church, at any rate, and I walked away from it again. This time I was an adult and my decision felt more considered and somehow definite.

Part of me wanted to go back to being one of the lads, back to what I knew, but however much I thought I wanted that, I couldn't do it. I couldn't go back to that lifestyle because, although I felt like the same old Terry Doyle inside, I had changed. I'd changed so much. I moved to the coast. It wasn't many miles from where I'd grown up but it felt more Bohemian, a place where running a tai chi class in the woods was seen as *de rigueur*. Teaching tai chi and meditation wasn't just a job to me; it was a way of life. I saw it as an adventure in which the more I learned, the more I had to share. I immersed myself in Buddhist retreats and signed up to go to Nepal as part of a fundraising trip to help build a small school and cottage hospital in the mountains.

The idea of visiting a place so different from England sounded fantastic, but, if truth be known, I was terrified. I'd never travelled. The furthest I'd been on holiday as a child was Scarborough, and it wasn't long before doubts about the trip set in. Who was I to be teaching people about these ancient traditions? I was born and bred in South Bank; what did I know? I tried to tell myself it would be OK, but fear began to rear its head in other ways. I became increasingly agoraphobic and scared of heights. I doubted everything, afraid that in trying to find myself I'd lost any sense of who I was.

In an attempt to cure myself of these irrational fears, a few weeks before the trip I drove out to the Lake District on my own. I wanted to experience being alone in the wilderness, or as much of a wilderness as I could imagine. So I parked up and I started to walk. I walked until I couldn't hear or see another person. To me, this place was the middle of nowhere, but being there didn't give me the liberating feeling I'd expected. Suddenly I felt very small and vulnerable. Shaking uncontrollably, I leant against a tree to steady myself, closed my eyes and pleaded, 'Please, God, help me feel your peace.'

When I opened my eyes again, it was like I was looking on a different world. The colours seemed more vibrant and I no longer felt lost. I felt part of my environment, rather than separate from it. The clouds, the trees, the water, the earth under my feet—there was a oneness about it all, and I was part of that. Some walkers appeared in the distance and I felt a great urge to run towards them and greet them with a hug. I didn't do it, obviously. That kind of behaviour can get you arrested. I wasn't crazy. I knew what I was doing. In fact, I was more lucid than I'd ever been—only I was euphoric, on an incredible high that lasted for about five days and gave me the courage to get on the plane to Nepal.

I know it sounds clichéd but my trip to the Himalayas was a life-changing experience. I guess sometimes we use clichés because they are true—or, at least, as true an expression as we'll find for something we can feel more than describe. I was moved by the Nepalese people. Compared with me, they had nothing materially, yet they had a depth of spirituality and happiness that I could only dream of. Whatever they had, I wanted a part of it.

My search for the happiness I'd witnessed in Nepal set

me off more firmly along the Buddhist path, so when I heard that the Dalai Lama was giving a talk in Manchester, I knew I had to be there. I felt lucky to get a seat near the front and, at the end, managed to talk to him, expressing my desire to convert.

'No need to convert,' he told me. 'Blossom where you are planted. Don't worry about dogma: simply be like Christ.'

As he spoke, something registered in me and it all made sense. It was as if I had come all this way to learn what I already knew, that the treasure I needed was there all the time, within my heart. Through his book *The Good Heart*, the Dalai Lama pointed me towards the World Community for Christian Meditation, of which he is a patron. I discovered that all of the practices I had been studying in Eastern faiths were there in the Christian faith too—mysticism, silence, contemplation, meditation—it was always there. I realised, with the same euphoria as I'd felt in the Lake District that day, that God is unconditional love and we're all a part of that love, all connected to each other and to every living thing. Life is a process of coming to realise that and realising that we are part of our old selves too.

I don't worry any more about who I am. Of course, I still get angry, I still get anxious and I still get fearful, but I don't dwell on those emotions like I used to. Meditation has taught me to sit with things, let things be and allow things to drop. I like to think about it as a glass filled with murky water. If you let it stand, eventually the sediment will settle. That is the difference in me today. If I get frazzled, I know that I can let it all go when I meditate. It's about trying to find the peace of the monastery while living in the marketplace. Lately, when I get cut up by another car on the road, I've noticed that I still experience a quick flash of anger in my solar plexus but then I think, no, don't bite, and I know that I've changed.

The old me is still there, only it's the me I probably always wanted to be. Being on a spiritual path, or whatever you want to call it, doesn't mean that I can't still enjoy football, music or a night in the pub. I can still go to the Boro match, but I don't go looking for trouble with rival fans and I don't cry like I used to if my team loses. I still go to the pub and enjoy the social aspect of it. Now I can have a few beers and I'm happy. Before, I'd drink that much at lunch time and go back to work.

My perception of happiness has changed, in that I don't chase the 50-inch plasma screen. I don't believe that material goods will bring me happiness. If I get something, I get something, but I know that the happiness that might come from having it is fleeting. I'm not interested in career and promotions like I once was. If these things happen, then so be it, but I don't chase them as I used to—going for another promotion to improve my status and because I thought it was what I had to do, rather than because I necessarily wanted the job.

There is a Zen proverb that I'm particularly fond of: 'When the pupil is ready to learn, a teacher will appear.' I've been lucky in that I've met some excellent teachers along the way, but perhaps that is because I was finally ready to learn. I still think about my dog, Prince. He taught me about unconditional love at a time when I most needed it. I lost him when he was knocked down by a car. He was still alive as I lifted him off the road. When he looked at me, I couldn't control my tears. He was dying, and, despite his pain, his eyes were still full of love for me. If only I had a tenth of that capacity to care for another living being. Now I see, that is what life is all about. It is about having the courage to open your heart and, if you get stung along the way, then so be it.

Of course, my philosophy doesn't come any easier to me than it does to anyone, but I try to be the eternal optimist. Yes, I've been hurt, but I need to dust myself down, lick my wounds and get out there again. Be vulnerable, take risks and let life be. Better to experience and live life than to look back in regret. I feel as if I've been on an adventure, and one that isn't over yet. I only hope I have the courage to live what I've learned—that happiness has always been within me and it's there for me to share.

Reflection

The Revd Hayley Matthews, Rector of Holy Innocents, Fallowfield, and Honorary Chaplain at St Peter's House, Manchester University

It's funny how much our search for God depends upon three things. First, creation—in Terry's case, just a wee puppy—reminding us that even if we live in an industrial area or a city centre, we are not cut off from creation if we choose to tend a house plant, never mind a pet.

Second, people—either denying or revealing the image of God in us. Are you a person of faith? Do all people feel God's love and acceptance of them in your gaze? Or do we make ourselves their God by judging them?

Third, a willingness to face being broken, for our hard outer shell of success and achievement and self-made glory to be seen for what it is.

It's a painful journey that we can only take if we are willing to allow ourselves to be vulnerable—to a dog's eyes, to an evening breeze, to our frail bodies that cannot keep up with our mind's relentless expectations as we drive ourselves to an image of a person that we think will be attractive to others, so as to prove our worth. Even people of faith fall foul of the idea that God loves them just as they are but more especially if they burn themselves out in his service.

What is beneath all of this striving, but our need to feel loved, to feel accepted as we are? Yet the irony is that only when we are at our weakest, feeling our failures crashing around us for all to see, do we grasp our acceptance by God and our own inestimable worth.

'Oh, that old chestnut,' I hear you thinking. 'Of course we need God when everything's going wrong. Where else would we turn? It's meaningless!' But don't get me wrong, we're not talking about the need for a crutch here, or the need for some kind of life-raft to get our precious goods and gifts back to the land we once strode through like giants. We're talking about the need to connect with the source of all love, the source of ourselves.

Yes, that's right, our 'selves'. Returning to our creator is the only way we see our true reflection: if we are made in God's image, then where better to look than to God for the template of what we were created to be? The world of 'success' and 'beauty' and 'brilliance' is just a hall of mirrors that changes with the eras and fads of our time, sometimes even with the company we keep, giving us not only a distorted view of ourselves but a distorted view of others and their intrinsic beauty and worth.

True beauty—vibrant, heart-moving life that courses through our bodies in waves of joy, or between the spirits of two human beings connecting on a far deeper level than words can convey—comes only from those true and time-less qualities that actually reflect the image of 'Emmanuel', God with us. These are the divine gifts of peace, joy and unconditional love, pointed out to us by every wag of a tail or dew-laden spider's web—love that keeps coming back for more, spring after spring, no matter how harsh the winter has been.

Often, we forget our core need simply to be valued for our very existence. Striving so hard to achieve the approval of others, from the time we take our first spelling test at school, somewhere deep inside we recognise that we are no longer simply being loved for having been born at all. We are now being expected to attain favour and approval. Even love is meted out in relation to our output. We slip from our higher calling as human beings into the quagmire of never-ending human doings.

When all is unravelling, we come to the place where God and humankind stand face to face—the place where we are known by our name. This is such an important part of the Christian faith: there is a God who knows us by name. Did you really hear that? A God who knows us not by reputation or accolade or sight, but by our name. God knows you, your 'self', for that is the most precious gift of all; that is your gift to the world, and God's gift to you.

If we think about what to 'give up' for Lent, perhaps it would be better to consider what is smothering us—which suits of armour need the heave-ho as all of our energy is spent keeping up the façade. We might think about our name and who we hear calling it—if anyone. Perhaps now is the time to listen for the still, small voice of calm. Could God really be calling *you* ?

You are loved, more than you could know. If you never gained another promotion or bore another child, cooked another meal or received another qualification, you – are – loved. And when you find that love reflected back to you from the heart of a God who continually whispers your name, so that you will be called back to your true self, made in the divine image, you will know peace. Jesus once said, 'What do you benefit if you gain the whole world but lose your own soul?'[3] And you know what? He was right. You are far too precious to lose, and he went out of his way to let us know that you are worth dying for. Don't throw that gift away.

What do you think?

- Who we are is so much more than the job we do, yet many times, like Terry, we don't think this way. Why is it so important to take this truth of life on board?
- Like many people, Terry found his life out of balance. What are the dangers of doing too much and how can we recognise it?
- Terry's recollection of his early experiences of church and religion was very negative. What factors that we can see from the story contributed to his feelings? Is this the whole picture?
- Terry's inability to share his knowledge of Chinese medicine with the congregation led him to label churchgoers as hypocritical. Would you agree with his judgment?
- 'Blossom where you are planted.' Terry travelled a long road from depression to inner peace. What helped him in this process?
- 'When the pupil is ready, the teacher will appear.' There are many teachers in our lives. Who or what have been the teachers in Terry's life? Are you able to recognise the teachers in your own life?
- 'We are all made in God's image.' What does that mean to you? How does that knowledge affect the way you think about yourself and your self-worth?

6

HIS NAME IS DAVID: GARY'S STORY

It was raining when I woke at 4 am. The sky was heavy with clouds and it didn't look as if the sun would show up any time soon. We were going to be in the fields all day and, if the weather didn't pick up, it wouldn't be much fun. Luckily we weren't camping. With three small children in tow, we had opted to spend our pilgrimage in a self-catering apartment. It was spacious and clean, part of an old country house. Looking out of the window, I felt we'd made the right choice, as it's an unfortunate truth that you can never rely on an English summer.

I comforted myself with the fact that there was still plenty of time before the rest of the family would be up. This was my regular prayer time, my time to be with God, to read his word, share my thoughts with him and be open to whatever he put on my heart for the day. I'd grown used to rising early and it had become a habit that even holidays couldn't break. This time fed my soul in a way that I couldn't explain. All I knew was that I felt better for it.

That morning, I prayed for the rain to stop and for the

powerful sunshine to come out and dry it all up. To continue with a wash-out like this would spoil our day for sure. Sometimes I wished that good weather was all I had to pray for, but God, more than anyone, knew we could do with some brightness in our lives at that time.

This wasn't the first time we as a family had visited the Shrine of Our Lady at Walsingham. For us it was a special place where we could be with friends and recharge physically, emotionally and spiritually. I needed that, and so did my wife, Zenka, who was almost four months pregnant and feeling more lethargic than she had when carrying our other three daughters. The events of the past year had taken a piece of her which I so wanted restored.

For months, our one-year-old daughter, Amelia, was falling forward and banging her head, often up to 30 times a day. We felt helpless, trying to cushion her falls with pillows but unable to anticipate every attack and prevent her delicate face from bruising. It was five months before doctors could tell us it was epilepsy and that it could be treated. In the meantime, we pleaded with God for healing. I told Zenka, 'God is not deaf. I've prayed for her—it's in his hands now.' I said the words but, as Amelia's symptoms continued, it was increasingly harder to believe them. At times I felt so miserable, weak and tired that I found it hard to pray.

I had put complete trust in God to heal our daughter. I'd heard that prayer was the single most powerful thing a human being could do. Prayer could change lives, stop wars, break addictions, heal people and even bring them back to life. In short, I believed that there was nothing that prayer couldn't accomplish. So when Amelia wasn't healed instantly, I felt angry and let down. For two days I refused to pray because I felt that God was watching all this happen but doing nothing to help.

Perhaps I had felt invincible because I'd already seen the power of prayer working in my own life. Even my non-believer friends would describe me as a walking miracle. Me, Gary Taffe, who ran away from an abusive home at 15 and into a life of addiction—who would have thought that God would turn my life around in such a way? So, if God could do that, which for most people would appear impossible, why couldn't he do this?

Once I calmed down, I was sure that God could cope with a bit of anger. My wife and I got angry with each other often enough—it didn't mean there was any less love between us. It's part of being in a relationship. I wouldn't be the first or the last to be angry with God.

That morning, as I watched the rain slide down the window, I wondered how many prayers God receives. I guessed an average of 160 million prayers an hour, which would work out at almost four billion a day. I didn't know what to make of this figure. Did God choose to answer some prayers and not others? Was mine four billionth on the list that day, and one too many? Or, for some reason, did my message just not get through?

After much thinking, I decided that however a situation appeared on the outside, I would be better to follow God and not my emotions. I told myself that, as the prophet Isaiah said, God's thoughts are not like my thoughts and his ways are not like my ways.[4]

When it was time to leave the apartment, the rain had eased to a slight drizzle. It wasn't ideal but nor was it bad enough to put us off joining the pilgrim group procession along the

'Holy Mile' from the Slipper Chapel into Walsingham. It was a slow, prayerful walk following some families who, like us, were pushing prams and buggies. There were also elderly pilgrims and many disabled people, some in wheelchairs and others on crutches: no one was excluded.

At the end of the walk, Zenka went to the Ladies and noticed some fresh blood. It was only a spot so I thought it would be OK, but later she started to feel unwell. I took the girls exploring in the woods so that Zenka could rest, and we were on our way back when one of our friends came running up to me to say that she had been taken to a doctor. I jumped in my friend's car and we drove to the surgery, but, because I had the girls with me, I had to wait outside until the doctor had finished his examination.

When Zenka came out of the consulting room, she looked tired. 'The doctor can't find a heartbeat,' she said quietly.

'But what do you think?' I asked

She looked at me and then looked down as if trying to wish away her reply. 'I think we have lost the baby.' Deep down I felt the same but kept hoping that when we got to the hospital, the next scan would reveal a pulsating heart and a new life. I wanted everything to go back to how it was that morning, when all I'd had to worry about was the rain.

I couldn't understand it. Only three weeks before, we'd seen the first scan of our baby, active and healthy. Sometimes, we told ourselves, with a very small baby it lies low in the womb and you don't always hear a heartbeat, but it doesn't mean the heartbeat isn't there.

The doctor at the hospital appeared to think so, too. After four hours of tests and scans, he could hear no definite heartbeat, but there was still hope, as a nurse told Zenka,

'We've got another better scanner. You can stay overnight or come back in the morning and we'll check again.'

While we were gone, word of our possible loss had spread around the camp. Everywhere we walked, people already knew and stopped us with hugs, kisses and comforting words. I grew up in foster care and had never experienced being part of an extended family. If I had to guess what it felt like, I'd say it was how I felt that day.

We had twelve hours before we returned to the hospital— twelve hours for a miracle. By coincidence, that night there was a healing mass in a big marquee near the shrine. My mind started piecing all the circumstances together. Surely, if God was going to perform a miracle, it would be here, at this site of pilgrimage among 3000 Christians. After praying at the healing mass, we would go for the scan in the morning and the baby's heart would be beating again. We'd come back and everyone would be raising their hands in high fives and singing hallelujah. God's glory would be seen and everyone who witnessed this miracle would retell the story to give great hope to others. This was going to be good for everyone. After all, for God, to start a heartbeat must be like switching on a light: in my childlike mind it was that simple.

The scan was set for 8.30am the next morning. Our good friend Liz and Zenka's cousin Ania agreed to look after the girls so that Zenka and I could both go and receive the news together. The nurse who greeted us was very jolly, which naturally took us by surprise. Given the circumstances, we had expected a more subdued welcome, and from the nurse's overt cheerfulness it was clear that she hadn't read the notes she was holding.

Zenka was invited to lie down on the bed, but the monitoring screen was in such a position that she couldn't see it. The nurse turned to read our file and I noticed her expression change, becoming serious. Then, with my full view of the screen, I saw our baby curled up, lying completely still.

After five minutes of running and pressing the scanner over Zenka's stomach, searching from different angles and positions, the nurse faced me. 'I'm so sorry,' she repeated over and over as she moved out of the room, leaving us alone.

I hugged Zenka and we both cried, knowing that our innermost thoughts had been confirmed. Our baby of four months had gone and the sadness hit me with an unexpected force. My child, my flesh and blood, dead inside my wife— how could this be? Why?

Thoughts flew around my head, so many in all different directions, and yet I said nothing. I felt alone, as if I'd been abandoned or forgotten. Why was God doing this to me? I wished I was free. Why did the Bible say we are free when it's not true, at least not for me? For months my life had felt like a permanent battle, with no rest mentally. Then, as quickly as that thought came, I got another, this time bringing with it a fleeting feeling of relief—relief that we did not have to go through the struggle of bringing up a fourth child. As soon as the thought came, I pushed it out, running from the idea. The pregnancy had been unexpected but I didn't know where such a thought would come from. What type of man was I even to think such things? How selfish, how awful! I didn't want to think like that; it was inhuman. I told myself that maybe these weren't my thoughts. After all, I couldn't honestly say what I was thinking, because I didn't know any more. As quick as one thought came, another replaced it.

In the car on the way back to the apartment, Zenka called some family members to tell them the sad news. I was pleased to be driving because it was something practical that I could do and it meant that I didn't have to talk. As we parked, I asked Zenka, 'Do you want to go home?' Without hesitation, she opted to stay for the final two days of the pilgrimage.

Back at the apartment, when I saw our daughters, a fresh pain grabbed me. I knew Amelia was too young to understand, but Mya, aged six, and Kasia, aged three, were expecting a new baby after Christmas. We had been talking about it with excitement for months. I went into the kitchen to prepare myself. I didn't want them to feel the pain that I held in my heart, but how could I shield them? How could I tell them what had happened, yet at the same time hold them and tell them that everything would be OK?

I knelt down, an arm around each of them, Mya and Kasia. Then, in the best way I could, I tried to explain that the baby—or, rather, their brother or sister who was due to arrive after Christmas—was no longer coming.

'The baby has gone straight up to heaven to be with God,' I said.

They looked at me bewildered before asking the unanswerable: 'Why, Daddy?'

That day felt unlike other days. The air was heavy with loss and I was aware that Zenka and I were acting differently. We were acting in the way people expected us to act at times like these; it was automatic, not purposeful.

We rejoined the pilgrimage. Some people, believing they were being nice, tried to persuade us not to give up hope, but by now we had accepted the loss. There was no turning back, no switching the baby's heart back on. However, there was a sense that people cared and we gained strength from that. It helped that they didn't ask, 'How are you?' when we didn't even know ourselves, but instead acknowledged our pain by saying, 'We are sorry; you're in our prayers.'

Sometimes there are no words, or we can feel that words are empty, but often the words that came, however few, weren't empty. I could see people reliving their own loss through our pain, as if we'd been invited into a secret world of miscarriage that I'd never been aware of. I was stunned at how many people, from close friends to a working security guard, were quick to admit their long-hidden pain for a baby they had lost. So many women came to me with tears in their eyes, revealing deep scars of past wounds, because now I was able to share their pain, to understand the similar heart-wrenching, life-changing scar that they lived with every day. All of these people had learned to live with their loss and I realised that, in time, we would too. Yet, while I knew we'd carry on, I wondered if we would ever be healed, and prayed to God to help us come through it.

That evening, a mass was offered up for our family. After-wards, a priest who we knew, Father Pat, asked if we had named the child, which we hadn't. It wasn't something that had crossed our minds, because we didn't even know if the baby was a boy or a girl. I was about to say this when Zenka said, 'Yes. If it was a girl we were going to call her Joy because the baby was so joyful on the first scan.'

Then I said, 'And David if it was a boy, because we talked about calling our second daughter David, if she'd been a boy.'

'Did you know that you can baptise an unborn child?' Father Pat asked. 'We can do that if you'd like.'

We didn't know about the 'baptism of desire', but it felt

right when Father Pat explained it as a non-water sort of baptism for those who had died before they were able to be baptised, so we agreed. We went into an empty marquee—a huge space for our small gathering, but at the time I didn't notice. We were all so focused on what was happening. There were six of us—me, Zenka, our unborn baby, Liz, Ania and Father Pat.

Zenka turned to Ania and said, 'I was going to ask you to be godmother, so you can be.' Ania nodded gently and agreed.

Father Pat made a sign of the cross on Zenka's tummy in water and oil. He then blessed us all and committed the baby to God. It felt as if we were doing something beautiful for this tiny person, a baby we wouldn't hold in our arms in this world but hoped to see in the world to come.

We decided to go home the next day, and I realised, once we were alone, why Zenka had been right to stay. We were weak in spirit and, for much of the pilgrimage, hadn't had the energy to pray, yet in a strange way it helped to know that so many others were praying for us. All the love, kind words and compassion we needed for healing were there among the other pilgrims. Back at home, though, our lives had changed and there was no escaping it.

The next morning, as always, I woke early to pray but I couldn't do it. I was angry. 'Lord, you said that whatever I ask for in prayer, I will receive if I have faith and believe. Well, I had faith. I believed in you. I did everything you asked but you haven't stuck to your side of the bargain. I've got a dead baby—I can't pray any more.' I slammed my Bible shut, got up from the chair, walked into the kitchen and stood, staring out on to the garden with adrenaline pumping through my body as if I'd just had a row.

It was Sunday. In a few hours I would be doing one of the readings at church. I couldn't do it in this frame of mind. Why, why, why, why, why? God could have saved our baby but he didn't, for reasons I would never know. Like a reluctant teenager, I prayed, 'I'm sorry, Lord. Help me to remember where I was before you stepped in and rescued me.'

Later that day, Zenka went to the hospital again. It was helpful to hear that there was nothing we could have done to have prevented the miscarriage. Sometimes it happens and no one, including the doctors, knows why.

The doctors gave Zenka a couple of options and she decided on medical management to speed up the process of the miscarriage. It meant taking some tablets, but she couldn't get those on a Sunday so would have to go back the next day. It was another waiting game.

I tried to appear as if I was holding it all together, but I was beginning to feel helpless. I couldn't even hold the thoughts in my head. It was clear that Zenka was tired and needed to rest, so I took the girls to the park and we walked and walked with no sense of the time.

When we got home, Zenka was sleeping, so I made food for myself and the girls and then put them to bed. At 9pm I was speaking to the hospital again. Zenka was in pain and said it felt like contractions. The nurse asked us to keep in touch by phone and told us that if Zenka had really heavy bleeding or couldn't cope with the pain, then we were to go to the hospital.

I went to a local garage to buy some painkillers and, when I got back, Zenka was arched over the sofa. The contractions were coming every three minutes, then every two. Zenka was still fully clothed, but every other aspect felt like a birth. I couldn't believe what was happening. Neither of us knew what to do. We hadn't known what to expect but we certainly hadn't expected this.

I got Zenka a glass of water and rubbed her back gently, just as I'd done when each of our daughters were born. 'I feel like I should push,' she said.

'Well, push then,' I offered, still not understanding what was happening but momentarily hoping that no blood would stain the carpet. At 11.45 pm, almost three hours after the first pains, Zenka looked at me. 'It's done,' she said. 'I have to go for a shower.'

I brought Zenka a towel, still trying to protect the carpet, and we hurried to the bathroom downstairs. I turned on the shower while she was undressing and, when I turned around, Zenka was standing in her underwear, holding a baby in the palm of her hand.

'We have a son,' she said, handing him to me gently. 'His name is David.'

While Zenka was showering, I examined him closely. I was amazed at how well formed he was. I could see his ears, his nose and mouth; his eyes were there too but they were filmed over. He had tiny arms and legs and I counted five fingers on each hand and five toes on each foot. Even his nails were visible.

Surprisingly I felt no fear, no anger or bitterness. I looked up and saw Zenka staring out of the steam-filled cabinet.

'You know I am at peace with this?' she said softly.

'Yes,' I replied. 'Me too.' Strangely, it was true. There we were in the middle of a heartbreaking moment and, while I did feel sad, my overwhelming sensation was one of peace.

I felt so strongly that we were not alone, as if someone or something was protecting us.

I made David a small bed out of an empty cardboard cappuccino box lined with white tissue paper and cotton wool. I couldn't take my eyes off him. It no longer felt as if we had had a baby. Rather, at that moment, I thought, 'We *have* a baby and he is real and he is here.'

We placed David on the coffee table and sat with him. I just wanted to enjoy being with him for a moment, to gain strength from that fleeting yet overwhelming peace which we had both experienced.

'Go with God, my son, and be blessed,' I whispered. 'Pray for us here—we love you very much. Until we meet again. Goodbye.' Some things in life happen and we can't understand why. No matter how long or how hard we pray about it, we never understand.

After a while I called the hospital. I was told to take Zenka to be checked out physically and to bring the baby as well. I called Liz and she came to watch the girls. Already we were back in a reality that no longer felt real. I drove while Zenka held David, who was in his cappuccino box bed in a carrier bag, on her knee. It was still dark when we pulled up. I often think of that night, walking through the car park and then along a maze of hospital corridors, holding a carrier bag with my son inside. Sometimes it's as if I was there but I wasn't, as if the whole experience was so overwhelming that I can only feel slices of what happened at any one time.

The staff at the hospital did much more than we could ever have expected. There were options, of which a funeral was one. The hospital organised it all and also helped us to put together a memory box, including an imprint of David's tiny but unique fingerprints. It is something we will always treasure—a small white box, wrapped with a yellow ribbon. There is a teddy bear inside, about 8–9 centimetres long, the size of David when he was born. We also included some personal memories—photographs of our daughters as they were at the time. Zenka wrote a poem to David, and Mya wrote her own small note: 'Dear David, we love you and we miss you. I'm sad that we are not going to see you and play with you, but we'll see you in heaven.'

The sun was shining as we buried David, but my heart was heavy. The service was short, with just me, Zenka and a priest. We said our final goodbyes. Zenka placed flowers on the tiny white coffin. On the top was a gold plate inscribed with the words, 'Baby David Taffe fell asleep'.

I placed my arm around Zenka. There was no escaping the sadness. 'I don't want the few short memories we have of David to be full of grief and regret,' I said. 'I want to feel satisfaction for the time that we did have together, to know that we have a son, his name is David and he is with God in heaven for reasons we don't understand.'

Our baby boy would have been three months old now. Only yesterday Zenka and I asked each other, with tears, why God would permit such things, such loss and suffering. It remains a mystery still.

One of the hardest things I've had to learn is to let go and let God take control—to say, 'OK, Lord I trust you to take charge of this, keep it or change it. I trust in you to make it right.'

There were times when it felt as if we had been abandoned, but, looking back, I can see how God strengthened us even when we weren't aware of it. At the time, we couldn't believe that we could lose a baby on a pilgrimage in Walsingham. It should have been the perfect place for healing, yet none came—at least, not the kind that restores physical life. Yet I'm glad that we stayed because we did find healing of a different kind, in the goodness and generosity of those around us. We couldn't pray but we gained hope from knowing that so many others were praying for us.

Zenka's giving birth to David when she did also came as a shock at the time, but if she had taken the medication in the hospital the following day, she would have been alone. I wouldn't have seen my son; I wouldn't have held him and loved him.

Perhaps the strangest thing I found was that through our loss we actually grew closer to God. How does that work? I don't know. All I know is that God repairs. He puts people together and keeps putting them back together when they fall apart: no one does it better.

Today, before I prayed, I read the parable of the two builders.[5] In it Jesus tells of a wise man who builds his house on rock. Wind, rain and floods shake the house but it doesn't fall. At the same time, another man, who built his house on sand, sees his home collapse under the same conditions. I thanked God for being my rock and foundation, for I've experienced much bad weather. At times it felt as if hurricanes and tornadoes had attacked my house, but it never fell.

Reflection
Canon Anthony McBride, Dean of Salford Cathedral

Whatever our loss, it is human to grieve it. However, as we all know, some losses are greater than others. The death of a loved one, although a natural part of life, is the greatest loss we will ever have to bear, and the death of a child brings with it so many more unanswered questions.

Grieving is a process, yet, no matter how familiar we are with the theory of the different stages, when it comes to our turn to grieve there is no easy way through it. Sometimes we may not realise what stage we are going through; we may get stuck, we may go backwards, but, whatever we are feeling in grief, we need permission to do so.

Anger is a natural part of grief, and often, for people of faith, this includes anger towards God. Christians often feel guilty about this, even though God is the one person we can be most angry with. While other people may get hurt by our anger, God will not. We can't harm God. He can absorb all the anger we care to throw at him.

It is natural at times of deep distress to feel as if we are losing our faith, because very often, in the worst situations, we find that we can't pray. Often this is because what we are describing as 'prayer' is what we did to praise God in the good times. During traumatic times, both our situation and our mindset change. In the psalms, we hear the sadness of the Israelites who have been exiled from their homeland. By the rivers of Babylon, they sit down and weep. Unable to sing the Lord's song in a foreign land, they leave their harps hanging on trees.[6] Even Jesus, in times of great suffering, found it an effort to pray in his usual way. As we read in Luke's Gospel, aware of the fate that awaited him, Jesus sweats blood as he prays for the suffering to be taken away.[7] These prayers, like ours in times of trouble, are of suffering—less a form of words than a cry of the spirit.

Sometimes, however, the feeling of being let down by God can be so strong, we find that we can no longer believe. We might pray to God to be happy, to be rich, to have a good family or for no evil to occur to us. But then, when something bad happens, we stop believing in God—and rightly so, because that God, as we have painted him, doesn't exist. After all, how could a loving God allow a child to die or any manner of other tragedy to occur? God isn't someone who decides that one couple is going to lose a child and another couple isn't. Our faith in God has to be just that—faith, with no certainty and no reason. We don't believe in God as the genie of the lamp, because, however much we might wish it, that sort of God doesn't exist. We believe in God who reveals himself through Jesus in a way that we could never imagine, in human form—and, like us, he suffered and he wept.

Jesus offers us unconditional love. Often, in times of trouble, although we may be too hurt to be aware of it, love is there with its quiet healing. The love we felt for the person we have lost lives on in our hearts; it never dies. Love is there too in the support of family and friends and practical help from the people around us. Those who have gone through similar experiences share yet another side of love, helping us to realise that we are not alone, giving us hope that we too can survive. Often the question then shifts from 'Why me?' to 'Why not me?' Am I not as human as the next person?

God isn't the God of the gaps, the person we substitute

for all things unknown. There are many things in life that we can't explain. Faith helps us to believe that those who have left this life have fulfilled a certain destiny, even if it is one we don't understand.

What do you think?

- Gary's faith journey followed an undulating path. Does this resonate with your own experience? Could you plot your own faith journey? Who or what helped you in your low moments?
- At his lowest points, Gary worried because he felt unable to pray. How did his experience make you think about prayer and what we are doing when we pray?
- After their loss, Gary and Zenka drew strength from the other pilgrims at Walsingham. How do you think local churches can support each other? In what ways does your local church reach out to others?
- Despite the depth of Gary's and Zenka's profound loss, they still found an overwhelming sense of peace, healing and closeness both to each other and to God. How was Gary's prayer eventually answered?
- The image we have of God will determine how we respond to him in times of loss. In the 'Reflection', there are three images of God that will not sustain us in times of difficulty. Can you identify them?
- Finding a quiet time in the morning to read his Bible and pray is important to Gary. In what ways do the prayers, rituals and practices of the Christian faith help those who are grieving?
- Where do we find sustaining images of God? Can you identify them in the 'Reflection'?

7

SEX AND NORMAL PEOPLE: CLAIRE'S STORY

Normal people don't sit at home watching porn on the internet. Well, nobody I knew would do that kind of thing, I was sure of it. So when I read headlines like 'One million UK adults addicted to online pornography' and 'Sex—the most searched-for word on the internet', I'd think, 'Who are all these men looking for sex online?' I supposed it could be women too, although, because I've never done it, I couldn't imagine any other woman wanting to either. Neither could I imagine any man who would. Those who did were gross perverts, obviously. As it turns out, I didn't have to look far to find one.

The topic arose not long after I got married. We'd come in from a night out and I was trying to explain my jealousy without sounding like a bunny boiler. Not that Simon would ever call me that—it was a label I was beating myself with. You see, I'd never had myself down as being the jealous type. I remember my best friend telling me how she hated it when her husband looked at attractive girls, and thinking, 'What's she talking about? He married her, didn't he? Why isn't she happy? What does she want? He's chosen her, so why be jealous?' Then I met Simon and I was just the same. All these feelings came out that I didn't know were inside me—feelings that I thought I'd never have—and I didn't know what to do with them.

Simon was my first real boyfriend. I'd never had a relationship that lasted more than two weeks—little holiday romances, nothing serious. We met through church. I was 28 at the time and had always felt quite happy being single. I never wanted to go out with someone just for the sake of it and it always seemed to be that the men I liked never liked me back. This time, the chemistry was on both sides and I couldn't quite believe it. Within six months we were husband and wife.

Although ours was a whirlwind romance by many people's standards, deep down I knew that getting married was the right decision. I was happy to be with Simon and only Simon for the rest of my life. Unfortunately, I wasn't prepared for the anxiety and insecurity that came with that commitment. I'd tense up if he looked at a pretty girl or chatted animatedly with a female friend. Other women were suddenly on my radar, and not in a friendly way. If I spotted a pretty girl, I knew that Simon must have noticed her too. My husband was being distracted by all these other women and I could do nothing about it. I stopped enjoying our nights out because every time Simon left me to speak to another woman, I'd be inwardly screaming, 'What about me?' I wanted to be the most important person in his life. Now we were married, why wasn't I? Of course, I never said this to Simon. Instead, I'd be irritable, we'd argue, and I'd end up feeling more anxious and rejected than I did before.

'I'm sorry. I don't know what's got into me recently,' I

finally admitted. 'It's awful, I feel so jealous and I don't know how to handle it.'

Simon smiled, 'I'd kind of guessed.'

'What? It's that obvious?'

'Yeah, just a little, but there's no reason to be.'

'I know that,' I smiled. 'I can't believe I'm behaving this way. I'm really struggling with it.'

I started to explain how I felt when we were out and how I hated myself for it.

'Hey, it's OK,' Simon comforted me. 'I've got my problems as well. I'm not perfect.'

'Like what? What do you struggle with?'

'Oh, you know, stuff.'

'Like what?'

'I'm just saying, don't beat yourself up. We've all got things we find hard.'

'Like what?'

'Claire, it's my struggle. I don't know what the big deal is.'

'The big deal? We're married now. If you're struggling with something, I want to be able to help. I want us to be able to talk about everything.'

'But there are some things you don't need to know.'

I felt like he was hiding something and started to push him for an answer. Then he told me. One of those men who looked at pornography on the internet was my husband.

'What the hell? I can't believe what you've just said. Why did you even bother getting married to me if you can just go on there and get your kicks off that?'

'Don't say that.'

'Well, what do you expect me to say? You're disgusting. It's like you're two-timing me.'

'It's not like that.'

'Well, what is it like then? Because that's what it feels like to me. How would you like it if I went on there looking at naked men?'

'I wouldn't like it.'

'So how do you think I feel, or don't you care?'

'Of course I care. It's not what you think.'

'So what is it then?'

He sighed loudly. 'I knew I shouldn't have said anything.'

'No, you'd rather just deceive me and let me think that I'm the one being unnecessarily jealous.'

'Well, you are. I'm not going off with someone else, I'm just looking at a bit of soft porn now and again.'

'What does that mean?'

'Well, there's some really sick stuff out there…'

'Oh, please…'

The louder I got, the quieter Simon got.

The argument didn't resolve itself that night. As much as it hurt me to hear Simon talk about his habit, I couldn't stop myself from repeatedly asking why he was doing it. Although it was uncomfortable for both of us, Simon did try to explain. Occasionally I could stay calm enough to listen to his reply.

There was no deceptive plan behind any of it. I didn't figure in his explanation at all, apart from the fact that we often kept different hours. I've always been an early bird, whereas Simon is a night owl. Most of the time I would be in bed when he looked at it. Simon told me that he'd be on the computer, a thought would come into his head and he'd just go with it. Unlike when he was a teenager, there wasn't that embarrassing moment of reaching for a top-shelf magazine and facing the newsagent. Now he could download porn at the click of a button. He didn't need to leave the house to find it; he didn't even need to get up from the chair. All he had to do was turn on the computer and he could sit at home and watch porn on the internet.

As far as Simon was concerned, it was perfectly normal. There was nothing seedy about it; he wasn't hurting anyone; no one else was involved. Yet who knew what had led those girls to sell their bodies for money? Maybe they wanted to do it, maybe they didn't. Did Simon ever worry about that? Probably not. Downloading those images into our home had sanitised and normalised them—in Simon's mind, at least.

I was angry. Angry that pornography was so mainstream. Angry that these images were in my home and I could do nothing about it. But, more than anything, I was angry that Simon wanted to look at other women in that way. I obviously wasn't the most important person in his life. If I was, he wouldn't do it.

I know that I was naive, but I wasn't completely closeted. I wasn't under the impression that when we said our vows a magic spell was cast so that we'd never find anyone else attractive again. Of course, I still find other men attractive. I can't help it if an attractive man walks past and catches my eye, but I wouldn't drift into a fantasy about going away with him on a boat or something. I wouldn't seek him out—and that is what hurt. Simon was seeking out other women, which just confirmed to me what I'd always felt—I wasn't enough.

'Look, I don't expect you to understand.' Now he was angry too. 'Sometimes I don't even understand. I don't want to keep doing it, but it's just there. It's so easy.'

'OK, so it's the computer's fault now. Well, throw it out of the window for all I care, because if I find you looking at that filth again, that's where it's going!'

Of course, he didn't stop, and I didn't throw the computer out of the window, although I threatened to many times.

For a while I found it difficult to be intimate. Was Simon thinking about those girls when he was with me? He never said so, but I felt that his internet habit was partly my fault. I wasn't attractive enough. Why else would he be looking at women on the computer when he could come upstairs and lie next to me? I might have understood it if I was away, but I was physically here and those girls weren't. They were a fantasy, someone nice to look at, who didn't answer back or say, 'Not tonight, honey.'

I imagined that those girls never wore dowdy clothes or had dull haircuts. They were never too rushed to put on a full face of make-up and never woke up with the previous night's mascara smudged under their eyes—whereas, look at me. I still dressed like a student, in jeans and sneakers, not like a wife, and certainly not like a woman who would attract attention. Who'd pay to see me naked? No wonder Simon was looking elsewhere.

I'd never felt comfortable in tight-fitting or revealing clothes, and the changing-room mirror didn't offer much support. Don't you think your legs look a little bit chunky in that dress? It's not the dress, love, it's your hair—and have you seen that spot, that red one there on the side of your chin? No new clothes are going to distract from that.

'How are you getting on in there?' the shop assistant asked.

'Oh, I'm not so sure it's me.'

'Let's see.'

Before I could object, she was adjusting the straps and

showering me with compliments. I didn't believe any of them, but obviously I had no idea what looked good and what didn't. Next thing, I was handing over my bank card and leaving with a bulging bag—my investment in a better me.

Just as I'd hoped, it didn't take long for Simon to notice the new Claire. Unfortunately, his reaction wasn't quite as I'd expected. 'You look different,' he said casually.

'Different? What does that mean? Is that good?'

'You look nice. It's just that I've not seen you wear clothes like that before. Where are you going?'

'Nowhere special. I just fancied a change.' There was a long pause before I added, 'I'm thinking of dyeing my hair blonde. What do you think?'

'If that's what you want, but I like your hair as it is.'

'You do? I thought you wanted me to change it?'

'Why?'

'Because I try to understand what you want, but it's like I'm getting mixed messages all the time. You say that you like me as I am, but your actions aren't showing me that.'

'What do you mean? What have I done to make you think I don't like your hair?'

'Well, those women you look at. They've got blonde hair.'

Cue another argument. I'd get upset; Simon would shut down. I'd get angry and end up shouting, 'Does our marriage mean anything to you? The way you are making me feel, it's like it's not important to you at all!'

At least once a month we'd have one of these head-to-heads. Everything would be OK for a while, then I'd start to worry and ask, 'Have you been on the computer recently?' He'd get annoyed that I'd asked, which came as no surprise.

I knew it would cause a row, but I had to ask nonetheless. If I held my feelings in, the resentment would end up coming between us anyway.

'I need to talk to you about it,' I'd insist, the stress in my voice making me sound stroppy.

'Yes, I have,' he'd admit.

I'd shout, he'd get defensive and shut down, and so it went on in a vicious cycle of anger and rejection. This carried on for many months until finally I voiced what I'd been feeling for some time, but was afraid to say. 'I can't go on like this, Simon. Something has got to change.'

Simon said nothing. I didn't want our marriage to end, but I was tired of shouting and not being heard. I needed someone to help me, to help us, but who could I turn to? What would I say? 'Oh, by the way, my husband's a porn addict, but I'm told not to worry about it because it's only soft porn.' I *did* worry about it. It had created a big black hole in our marriage. It had made me mistrustful of my husband and uncomfortable with my friends. Everyone could tell that there was something bothering me, but I couldn't be honest about what it was. I couldn't talk about it because to do so would feel like a betrayal, although I was beginning to feel that there wasn't much of a relationship left to betray.

I didn't want to tell people because, when someone mentioned Simon, I didn't want them always to add in their mind '…the porn addict'. Or was that just me? I didn't know what anyone else thought about pornography because I never spoke about it. I didn't know anyone who talked about it, except comedians on TV. I'd cringe when anything like that came on, and so often it was presented as if it was all a big joke—a joke that I didn't get.

After much thought, I asked Simon, 'Can I speak to some-one else? Because I'm struggling to know how to deal with this.' There was a long pause. Neither of us wanted another row, but it had taken a lot for me to admit I needed help, so I continued. 'Simon, I'm serious. I need to speak to someone. I don't know who. Maybe your dad?'

'No! My dad? No way.' He was adamant.

'OK, not your dad, but I need to tell someone. Is there someone I can speak to?'

'If you really need to speak to someone, I suppose it's all right,' he muttered.

Neither of us spoke for a few minutes. To break the awk-wardness of the silence, I went to make a drink and handed it to Simon with a reconciliatory smile.

'Thanks.' He took a sip. 'I know what I just said, but I'd rather you didn't tell anyone.'

'I'd rather not talk about it either, because it's just em-barrassing,' I said, screwing up my face in mock disgust, and we both laughed. 'Seriously, though, what are we going to do, Simon? I need to know how I can help, because me getting all hysterical isn't helping either of us.'

'I don't want to hurt you, Claire.' His tone was generous and I believed him. 'I'm not doing it on purpose to get at you. I want to do the right thing, but it's a battle. I'm not the only guy that looks at these things. Ben at church—he's had a problem with it.'

'You didn't tell him about us, did you?' I said, suddenly panicked.

'No, of course I didn't. He was just saying that it was a struggle for him, and his wife has been really supportive.'

That comment hit me hard. Simon must have seen me

flinch, but I was determined to stay calm. 'In what way?'

'She just said, "Aw, hun, I'll pray for you."'

How could she say that? How could she say, 'I'll pray for you'?

He continued, 'She suggested that he speak to the vicar about it, who told him, "When you sit down at your computer, ask God to be with you."'

'That was it?'

'Yeah. After three months of asking God to be with him, he felt sick doing it.'

Simon obviously took that as an encouraging thing. I didn't know what to think, so I just said what I felt. 'If I was doing something that upset you in a similar way, or even in a different way but it was really upsetting you, I'd hope that I could change or get the help I needed to work with you to try and stop doing whatever it was.'

'Yeah, totally,' he agreed.

'Do you want to stop?'

'Yes.'

'You mean that?'

'Of course.'

'So, what can I do to help?'

'Asking me every couple of weeks isn't the best thing. You make me feel really guilty, and the pressure kind of makes it worse.'

'Are you saying it's my fault?'

'No.'

'I don't understand. I don't want to make it worse but I don't know what I can do to help.'

'I don't want you to ask me again.'

'I don't know if I can do that,' I admitted. 'I don't want

you to be hiding. Even if you're not doing anything, I'd always be wondering, and I can't live like that. I can't live without trust. I can't live any more with secrets between us.'

Simon thought for a moment. 'You're right. I hate seeing you upset like this. If it's something I'm embarrassed about saying to someone, then it's something that I need to be accountable for. I don't want to talk to anyone else, but you can ask me and I'll tell you the truth. Just don't ask me all the time.'

'What if I asked you once a month?'

'Yeah, that's fine.'

So, that's what we did. On the first day of each month, Simon told me how he was getting on. The idea was to help him to be more self-controlled when he was on the computer. If he looked at those sites, he knew that he would have to account for his actions later on. When he switched on the computer, he would have to think beyond the here and now. He might be alone but he needed to understand that what he was doing had an impact on other people. He had to think about how I would feel when he told me.

At first I found it hard not to react angrily, particularly when months went by without much change. My instinct was to yell, 'You're horrible. You disgust me. Is there any good in you?' But where was the grace in that? If I really wanted to help Simon, then I had to judge him less harshly. It wasn't about condoning what he was doing, but about realising that my husband was more than his pornography addiction. That one issue had clouded all my thoughts about him. I needed to start seeing his good points again, to see the Simon I fell in love with and realise that this problem, as much as I hated it, was only a small part of who he was. I needed to accept that it was his problem, not mine. I needed to let go. I wasn't the one addicted to pornography. I couldn't stop for him. He had to do that himself and I was glad that he wanted to change, even if I couldn't always see much evidence of it. What kept me going were the glimmers of hope that his habit wasn't quite as extreme and, rather than freaking out at every admission, I'd look forward to small achievements. The first time he went a whole month without using the computer in this way, we were both so happy.

Life changed again once we had children. We were both focused on looking after them as best we could and less concerned about examining any problems that we might have as a couple. It's not that we weren't interested in each other, but I stopped trying to sort him out. I stopped taking everything he did personally. My priorities changed. I became more relaxed about how I looked, and I think Simon also felt that he could be more himself, without me breathing down his neck, trying to mould him into a different type of person.

Over time, our monthly chats became less accusatory on my part and less defensive on his. We never ignored the issue but we began to use the time to talk calmly about other problems we were having and to think about where we might be able to support each other better. Afterwards we would pray together, asking God to give us the strength to overcome whatever struggles we'd discussed.

During this time, I told Simon about the recurring nightmares I was having and how they had left me feeling low. I couldn't see any reason behind them, but, as I explained how I felt, Simon began to see a connection between him telling me he'd been using the computer to look at pornography and me having the nightmares. This realisation upset Simon more than all my screaming and shouting had done. I didn't need to say anything: he could see how much his actions were affecting me, and it strengthened his resolve to change.

The connection he made came as a surprise to me too. It wasn't that I was intentionally harbouring resentment towards him, but choosing to forgive Simon didn't remove my memory of his actions or stop them from hurting me. In this sense, forgiveness wasn't a feeling. It was about me making a decision to value our marriage more than this one issue. It was a commitment to love and accept Simon in spite of his actions that disappointed me. Forgiveness didn't remove the consequences of hurtful actions in our marriage, but it allowed us to stay connected so that our marriage could survive.

At one time, Simon's habit was everything to me. I couldn't see past it, even though there were other things in my life and in our relationship that needed attention. I hope that I can do that now. You can't build back trust overnight. It takes time, but it's growing all the time and I am able to see the good in Simon, despite the blips.

Occasionally I'll type something into the computer and its history automatically suggests pornographic websites for me to look at. These choices appear even if I type in something innocent. When that happens, I don't wait for the first of the month to bring it up, but I try to stay calm. I don't want to see those sites—even the names of them—and I don't want our children to see them either. As they get older, their use of the computer will probably change the way I react to Simon's slips again. Recently I asked what he thought about getting a porn blocker on the computer so that the children can't click on to unsuitable sites accidentally. He said, 'If you want to,

I'm happy with that.' We haven't done anything about it yet, but knowing that he doesn't mind me installing something like that makes me realise how far we've come.

After ten years of marriage, I'd like to say that my husband never looks at pornography on the internet, but I can't. We've not got to the place where we hope to be, but where we are is a big improvement on where we were. Simon has joined a support group for men who want to stop using pornography. Hearing other people's experiences has helped me to put our problems in perspective and to see our relationship in a different light. I still don't like to talk about Simon looking at pornography, but neither do I feel so isolated and ashamed by it. I know that there are many other young men struggling with the same issues, men who want to change and to have someone to support them while they're changing.

As for our marriage, we keep growing together and asking God to give us the grace for each day, because in any marriage, however good, I've come to realise that there will always be something for either partner to get upset about. The secret is not to dwell on those things, and to keep going. Thankfully, we are moving in the right direction.

Reflection

Dr Thaddeus Birchard, founder of the Association for the Treatment of Sexual Addiction and Compulsivity Clinical Director, Marylebone Centre for Psychological Therapies

The Marylebone Centre for Psychological Therapies was founded in 2001. As a clinic we specialise in three things: distressed relationships, mood disorders and human sexuality. In the latter category we have developed a programme of treatment for men with compulsive patterns of sexual behaviour. It is partly on this basis that I write. I am also an Anglican priest, although not working now in parish ministry but rather in psychotherapy—the other 'cure of souls'.

The term 'addiction' comes from the Latin *addicere*, which means something like 'to bind over by judicial decree'. In other words, addiction means becoming a prisoner to a seemingly unavoidable and repetitious pattern of behaviour. Sexual addiction is characterised by four criteria:

- The behaviour is preoccupying and feels out of control.
- People try to stop but find that they cannot stay stopped.
- The behaviour brings with it harmful consequences—in Simon's case, the immense distress caused to his wife and the threat his behaviour posed to the continuation of the relationship.
- Most importantly, the behaviour has a function, which is normally to anaesthetise some chronic or acute negative feeling state. This behaviour is reinforced by sexual pleasure, probably the most powerful of all human reinforcing mechanisms.

There is also a biological event going on. The evolutionary biologists point out that, in our species, women attract and men are attracted. The male goal is to maximise the spread of his DNA and this makes him automatically alert to notice attractive women. He is not doing anything bad: he is just being human. Women, on the other hand, have a different biological strategy. The way they maximise their DNA is to find one man who will have the resources to look after them and their children. This biological difference explains the distress and upset caused to women when men use pornography. It also explains a difference in computer use. Men use it to look at women and body parts. Women who use the internet tend to use chat rooms. As the saying goes, 'Men have relationships to have sex, and women have sex to have relationships.'

There is a tendency, these days, to call everything an addiction. We meet many men with a pattern of behaviour similar to the one given in Claire's narrative, but I always have to ask, does the behaviour fit the criteria for addiction? Sometimes it does and sometimes it does not. There is a fine judgment to be made. Are we dealing with ordinary male behaviour or are we dealing with sexual compulsivity? Ultimately, only the man himself can make that judgment.

What do you think?

- Pornography is often the butt of jokes and is considered by some to be a 'private occupation' that doesn't affect anyone else. Do you agree with this point of view?
- Shame can be both crippling and motivating. What is the evidence for both of these responses in Claire's account?

- What do you find surprising and inspiring about this couple and their relationship?
- Children can bring about a positive change in a relationship. What positive changes do you see children bringing to the relationship of the young couple in this account?
- 'Men have relationships to have sex. Women have sex to have relationships.' Do you agree with this statement?
- A person whose partner is involved in pornography may change his or her appearance and behaviour in order to become seemingly more attractive. Does this indicate that, at some level, they feel responsible for the behaviour of their partner?
- What part does forgiveness play in this relationship?

8

THE PRICE OF BEING RIGHT: JAMES' STORY

It's hard to explain why I stopped speaking to my brother, Tom. We had a fall-out but, from that day to this, I don't know what it was all about.

It was summer and one of those sunny days in England that we call too good to waste. Tom has always been a keen driver and, as I don't drive, he called to see if I fancied a trip out. From the window I saw his Peugeot drive around the corner and I was outside waiting when he pulled up. His wife, Sarah, was in the passenger seat and I sensed they might have had a few cross words. Whatever the reason, Tom seemed to be in a bit of a mood, but neither of them mentioned it so I didn't either. We drove across town to pick up our sister, Carolyn, and, once there were four of us in the car, the mood lifted considerably.

As the conversation started to flow, Sarah suggested that we make the most of the sunshine and have a picnic. It sounded a grand idea, except that none of us had brought any food. Not to be put off, Tom said he knew where we'd find a supermarket nearby. He took a quick detour, turning down a narrow lane as a souped-up car whizzed by at what felt like a dangerous speed.

'Woah!' I said, aiming my comment at the recklessness of the other driver.

'Oh, what the hell's up with you?' Tom fired back. 'You're worse than an old woman.'

I tried to explain that I'd thought the other car was going to hit us, but he didn't want to listen. Still, he was right about the supermarket and it was only a couple of minutes before we pulled up outside. Sarah and Carolyn went inside to buy food and I stayed in the car with Tom. I tried to make conversation but he didn't pick up on anything and we sat in silence. Thinking I might as well do something useful, I said, 'I'm going to get a lottery ticket.' Tom didn't reply, so I got out and walked across the car park towards the kiosk.

The sun had obviously enticed people out of their houses to make the most of the day, because the shop felt even busier than usual for a Saturday morning and I had quite a long wait at the till. Getting back in the car, I let out a sigh of relief: 'Wow, the queue for that...'

Before I could finish the sentence, Tom swung his head round and interrupted. 'Listen, you. You're too familiar.'

'What? What are you talking about?'

'You know,' he snapped.

I didn't know what he meant. I'm not sure he meant much at all, but it was clear that he had the needle with something and I didn't want to spend the rest of the day at the sharp end of it. 'I can't be doing with this, Tom,' I said, opening the car door to leave. 'You're mad. You drive me mad.'

Adrenaline added an unusual speed to my stride and it wasn't long before I was standing at the bus stop across the road. I just wanted to get home, but what about Sarah and Carolyn? They were still in the shop, and I didn't want them to be buying food for me that I wouldn't eat. I dashed back and, the crowds being what they were that morning, they were still inside. When Sarah saw me, she noticed straight away that something was wrong. I tried to explain but she laughed it off. 'Oh, you brothers!'

Her flippancy annoyed me. If was as if Tom could do and say whatever he liked and that would be OK, because that's just how he was. Why did no one ever say, 'You're out of order there, Tom'? Well, if they thought I was going to get back into the car as if nothing had happened, they could think again.

'No, I've had enough of him speaking to me like that. I'm going home. He drives me mad. He is nuts.'

Sarah tried to talk me round, but I didn't want to hear any more excuses for Tom's moods. 'Leave me alone.' I was serious now and she could see it. 'I don't want to know.' With that I turned and left.

So, that was our fall-out. When I tell it like that, it doesn't sound much of a reason to stop speaking. Like I said, I still don't know what it was all about. To me it was another example of how Tom didn't treat me as a brother should, or at least how I thought a brother should behave.

Having an older brother in school was often seen as an advantage, but not for me. My glasses were always buckled from being knocked off, but Tom never took my part. He never stuck up for me like my friends' brothers did for them. In some ways I'm glad he didn't, because, despite my glasses, I could use my own strength enough when it mattered. Not against Tom, though. He was always bigger than me and would often give me a good pasting. Growing up, we were always fighting, acting as if we hated each other. At times we probably did—and, as ridiculous as it might sound at my age, whenever we argued as adults, in my mind it always came back to the playground.

It was a long time since we were children, but Tom still knew how to hurt me. Well, I wasn't going to allow it any more. I didn't have to live under the same roof as him and I didn't have to put up with his whims. As I shut the car door behind me that day, something inside me hardened. It wasn't that I didn't love him, but I didn't want to be hurt by him any longer. It was sad but my mind was set.

At the time of the fall-out, I'd not long retired and had recently moved house. We now live about an hour away from each other. It isn't a great distance but it is far enough not to bump into each other out and about. Perhaps the fall-out wouldn't have got so out of hand if we had lived closer together. If we saw each other on a regular basis, the barriers would've been broken down more easily, if for no other reason than that we'd have got fed up of the fight—or, in our case, the silence. As it was, we grew further and further apart. The idea that the space would make us think better of each other, that absence would make the heart grow fonder, was a load of old cobblers. The space only gave me time to ruminate on all of Tom's bad points, on why I was right not to speak to him, on how many times he had hurt me in the past, on why I didn't need him in my life. It made me realise how different we were. He likes sport; I like partying. He's a home bird; I like travelling. He likes security; I like adventure. I think about how my words might affect people; he says what he likes, when he likes, with no thought for the consequences. I suppose he'd always been like that. Perhaps when I was working I was too busy to notice, or perhaps it was about time I said, 'Enough is enough.'

In all my thoughts about our fall-out, I never really considered the consequences of deciding I wouldn't speak to Tom—at least, not beyond the initial consequence of saving myself from his, at times, vicious tongue. I certainly never imagined that the silence would go on for nearly as long as it did. At the same time, I hadn't done anything wrong. If anyone was going to apologise, it should be him—but Tom didn't apologise and, the longer we didn't speak, the more it became an issue that we didn't speak.

For years we ignored each other like that. We could be in the same room and it was as if we didn't know each other. Well, it was worse than that because, unlike strangers, we would purposely avoid each other where we could, and where we couldn't we were determined not to speak, averting our eyes if we knew the other was there. At family celebrations, we could be sitting at the same table with a conversation going on around us and we wouldn't share a word. Once I went to the Gents, saw Tom at the urinal and walked out. I'd be in pain rather than risk talking to him again.

I soon came to learn that it takes real effort to maintain the initial intensity of a fall-out. Anger is energy-sapping, and inevitably it starts to impinge on our capacity to love. Of course, it's hard to see that when your heart is the one being consumed by a fight. After a while the constant upset, distance between us and methods of avoidance began to feel normal. To speak to Tom would have felt strange; it wouldn't have felt right. By now, everyone knew us as the brothers who didn't speak, and that was how it would be.

When our sister Carolyn was seriously ill in hospital, I would find out from other family members when Tom and Sarah would be visiting and make sure that I avoided those times. Carolyn was very heavily sedated. She was breathing but that was about all she could do: she couldn't eat or drink on her own. I'd visit most days, going through the process of putting on a gown and making sure I'd sterilised my hands before entering the intensive care unit. I'd talk to her about my day and about people we both knew—except Tom, of course. I never mentioned Tom. He was our brother but I acted as if he didn't exist.

Carolyn couldn't respond to me, so I made up conversations in my head. I wanted her to feel that everything was all right, for her to believe that I wasn't worried by all the tubes and monitors. I don't know how well I pulled it off. It was hard to see Carolyn like this. She'd always been so lively. I guessed that she was dying, although I didn't want to admit it. There wasn't much that I could do for her, so I'd do small things like dipping cottonwool buds in lemon-flavoured balm and rubbing it on her lips to moisturise them.

One afternoon, after I'd smoothed the balm on her lips, I stepped out of the room to see Tom and Sarah walking down the corridor towards me. Why hadn't someone told me they were coming? Why would they turn up unexpectedly like this? 'Oh, hello,' I said, unable to hide my surprise. 'I'm just about to go.'

'No, you don't have to go,' Sarah replied.

'I've been here long enough.' It was the truth: I'd been there 50 minutes, which was why I was taking a break. At least I hadn't bumped into him in front of Carolyn. Goodness knows she didn't need that in her condition. 'She's out of it; she's been sedated,' I added, although, since they'd been visiting, they probably already knew. 'I have put the moisture on her lips.'

'Do you want to talk?' Tom asked.

I knew that it was his way of apologising, but I rejected it with a gentle 'No' and walked off. I didn't feel able to talk. Those few words we had were painful enough. Talking to Tom felt wrong. It wasn't fair to use Carolyn's illness to rub out what he had done. I was so upset by the whole situation—about seeing Carolyn so ill, and being caught unawares by Tom's presence. It wasn't that I didn't recognise his gesture. I did, but I didn't feel strong enough to accept it, and, because I didn't, the silence went on.

Carolyn didn't live to see us on speaking terms again. Even her funeral couldn't heal the rift that had become so deep between us. Family funerals, like weddings, were events that neither of us could reasonably avoid. Unfortunately, at our age the funerals come around far more frequently than is good for anybody. Sometimes, when I think back over my life, I find it hard to believe that so many of my friends aren't beside me any more. I tell myself, 'Keep going, Jimmy. You're still here, lad; you're doing something right, just keep going.'

I think back to when we were young, when Tom was there and we were scrapping like raggy-bottomed waistcoat tearers. Funerals have a habit of doing that to you—rooting out all your grief so that you mourn for the person who has passed and all the others who have gone before. Sometimes we mourn for the living as well as the dead, but we have to keep going as best we can, and my life didn't include Tom any more.

Seasons came and went. The pain of our fall-out didn't go away; I just learned to live with it better. I knew I'd done nothing wrong, so I didn't see that there was anything I could do to improve our relationship. I needed to accept it, and I thought I had, until another funeral would rake it all up again.

This time it was for our cousin Enid, someone else we grew up with, someone else who'd shared our childhood. As always, Tom and I carefully avoided each other as we walked into the church, knelt to pray, stood by the graveside and offered our condolences to the family. Our actions had become so habitual that I barely thought of Tom—not until the reception, when his daughter, Vicky, came over to talk to me. That in itself wasn't unusual. Although I didn't speak to her dad, we'd never ignored each other and I was grateful to her for that. After all, it wasn't our fight.

'Hello, love. How are you?' I said, reaching out to welcome her with a hug.

'Uncle James, enough is enough.'

'Hey, come on now.' She was crying and I didn't know what to say. It hurt me to see her like this, as if the day wasn't sad enough as it was.

'No. It's not OK. I've never said anything about you and my dad, but it's upsetting everyone and I've had enough of it. When we have parties and get-togethers at Christmas and birthdays, you're never there because of the argument you had, and that's not right. You were always there, and you should be there. Don't you think it's about time you made up?'

'Look, I've got to go,' I said, trying to avoid the issue. 'I have, really. I'm on the train.'

'Well, you'll have to miss your train because you're not going from here until you get friendly.'

'I'm sorry, love, I can't.'

'She's right, you know, James.' It was George Johnson, who had been a friend of the family for years. 'Can't you bury the hatchet with Tom?'

I didn't answer him but I listened to what he had to say.

'Go on,' he encouraged me. 'I don't know the ins and outs of it, but does it matter? I'm not saying you're in the wrong, but look at the girl. What is it costing you to be right?'

George was a man I had always respected. He wouldn't say something like that glibly and I knew it. He wasn't pretending that my beef with Tom was over nothing. If it was nothing, he wouldn't have interfered at all. If it was nothing, it never would have gone on for as long as it did. Yet, in all my hurt, I'd never thought about how my relationship with Tom affected anyone else. In my mind it was always between me and him. Now I could see how wide our rift had become, how many other people it hurt and continued to hurt. I'd never meant for this to happen. I was always so worried about attending events where Tom would be, worried about my own reaction, about how I could avoid him, that there was no time to think about anyone else.

I looked up and saw Tom. It had been six years. What do you say after all that time? I didn't know, but I felt all eyes fix on me as I walked across the room towards him. I had to ignore them, pretend there was no one else there. After all, I'd grown used to that.

I was sure that everyone could feel the tension in the room. Tom knew I was coming his way and, for once, he didn't try to move.

'Aye, aye,' I said.

'Aye, aye,' Tom replied.

'I've got to go, Tom,' I said, holding out my hand in friendship. 'Anyway, I'm just shaking hands with you to say I'll talk to you later. I've got a train to catch, but I just wanted to say I'll have a word with you.'

We never did have a conversation about why we didn't speak for all those years, what really went on in our heads that day of the fall-out, why he never stuck up for me as a child, or the reasons behind so many arguments and fights we'd had over the years. If we did try to talk about those things, I suppose it would only start another row.

These days, he can't do enough for me. He will run me anywhere in his car. If I'm unwell, he'll say, 'I don't care what time it is, James, you must ring me.' He means it, too. I know if I ever needed anything, Tom would be there. He'd drive an hour in the middle of the night if need be, and he wouldn't complain about it. That said, he still annoys the hell out of me sometimes. He's not diplomatic one bit, and I guess, at his age, he never will be. In my view, we've got a brain and we should think before we open our mouth. Not Tom. Whatever is on his mind, he'll come right out with it, never thinking, 'Am I going to hurt you?' And of course, he does still hurt me. I don't accept being spoken to as if I'm worth no more than the dirt on his shoe, but I don't let it fester, for my sake as much as his.

Perhaps, even though I can't see it, I hurt Tom too in different ways. He wouldn't ever show it: he's straight on with the next thing, and I've noticed that he doesn't bear grudges, as odd as that may sound. Like I've said before, we're different people. He drives me mad, but he's my brother and I love him.

Reflection

The Revd Julie Martin, United Reformed Church minister

Walls and barriers are hard to break down, especially when they have grown bit by bit. Some walls, like the Berlin Wall, are put up overnight. They stay in place for many years, causing misery to those caught on either side of them. Then suddenly they come down. But even this requires hard work and courage. The decision to take the wall down is a brave one. The act of taking it down needs strength and the right tools.

Barriers that have grown slowly can be, like hedges, intricately woven together. Hammers will not knock them down. The layers have to be pulled apart or cut back slowly. A helping hand may be valuable to give guidance and support.

Most of us have walls and barriers in our lives. Often they have become so much a part of who we are that we take them for granted. We may or may not remember how they first came into existence. Other people may or may not be aware of them and the effect they are having on our lives.

The decision to put up a barrier may be taken deliberately, as happened with the Berlin Wall. In other cases, though, the cause lies in a seemingly insignificant event. A relationship starts to break down and the consequences then spiral out of control. It seems easier to live with the barrier than to dismantle it.

People look in all sorts of places for words of wisdom about breaking down such barriers. The insights of psychology can help, as can the experiences of others. Phrases come into our minds, urging us not to go to bed angry[8] and not to complain about the small speck of dust in our brother's eye while ignoring the large plank in our own.[9] To people of faith, these words may have special significance, because they come from the Bible, but there is a universal truth in them too.

The need for forgiveness is also universal. The Bible speaks of a God who loves and accepts and forgives. This God asks us to forgive those who have wronged us, which is not always easy to do. Yet, not to forgive may be the worse option. Bitterness grows and the burden remains. The wall or barrier may get higher and seem even more insurmountable.

Forgiving those who have wronged us is difficult. So too is forgiving ourselves, especially if, deep down, we realise that we have played a part in putting up the barrier. It may be an exaggeration to say that we have a plank in our eye, but there could be a few specks of dust preventing us from seeing things clearly. Removing the dust may improve our vision.

If forgiving ourselves is difficult, then loving and accepting ourselves may be even harder, yet the one may lead to the other. Another barrier may come down and our perspective on life may change. We gain a wider view on what is happening. Other advantages follow. When the Berlin Wall came down, many reunions were possible.

Walls and barriers do not have to be permanent. The decision to remove one may not be easy, but it is a decision worth taking.

What do you think?

- James knew that Tom was 'in a mood' on the day of the fall-out, yet he still reacted very negatively to Tom's comments. Why do you think that he had such a strong reaction?

- Was Tom at fault for not living up to James's expectations? Think about how the expectations you have of people affect your relationship with them.
- James comments that 'anger is energy-sapping, and inevitably it starts to impinge on our capacity to love'. Is this always the case?
- The longer the silence went on, the deeper the rift between the brothers grew. Why do you think this was?
- James acknowledged that he hadn't given any thought to the way his relationship with his brother affected others. What impact do you think it had on their family and friends?
- By the end of the account, have the brothers demonstrated that they have changed? How would you account for this?
- What part does forgiveness play in this tale? Could others have helped to bring about reconciliation at an earlier stage?

9

THE PATH IS MADE BY WALKING: YOUR STORY

Forgiveness is the attribute of the strong.
MAHATMA GANDHI

Whether you are aged ten or are nearing 100, at many points in your life you will have forgiven and been forgiven. Often, the act of forgiveness in our lives goes barely noticed, seen simply as a normal part of life's rollercoaster. At other times, forgiveness becomes so difficult that it seems impossible. At such times, we don't want to become trapped in a cycle of resentment and bitterness, but we don't always know how to escape it. Wherever you are in your life right now, thinking about your own experience of forgiveness can help you to make this gift an everyday part of your life.

In this final chapter you will find a series of questions that are best worked through individually, after which you may like to share your responses with a group of people you trust. Sometimes it is hard for us to see the bigger picture in our own life. When we are hurting, it is difficult to imagine how we will ever recover from life's pain and setbacks. Often it is easier to see from the outside where help might come from, where hope is burning and where God is working, however silently, in other people's lives. As each of the stories told in this book has demonstrated, help does not always come from where we expect it, and sometimes it is only with hindsight that we are able to recognise the positive significance of events or people in our lives. Being open to forgiveness means being open to love, wherever it appears. This is never easy, particularly not after we have been hurt badly, but, if we are not open to love in all its forms, we may not always recognise the support that could eventually help us to heal.

The people who shared their stories for this book all felt, at one point, as if they were stuck in a cycle of pain. Healing takes time and there is no magic formula to calculate how long that might take. However, at some point in each testimony there was a leap of grace and their lives were restored through the power of forgiveness. That leap of grace can happen for you too. Of course, that doesn't mean that you will necessarily forget the things that have happened in your life that require you to forgive or to seek forgiveness. None of the people in this book forgot what had happened to them, but they were able to move forward, to keep turning the pages of life, in search of a better ending.

The idea that we can 'forgive and forget' is a myth that sadly prevents many from enjoying the benefits of forgiveness and looking to the future with hope. It has become common for people to describe anything from the most terrible crimes to a cross word between friends as being unforgivable. Perhaps what they really mean to say is that the consequences of what has been done or said cannot be erased. Even with genuine forgiveness, we cannot go back and undo what has been done. Rather, in forgiving, we choose not to dwell on the hurts of the past and on questions that can never be answered. Instead, we learn to focus on our life now, remembering that there is more of our story still to come. Forgiveness cuts our ties to a painful past and gives us the freedom to make the most of our future. In order to enjoy that future, we need to keep moving forward, to tread our own path of forgiveness. I hope the questions below will encourage you to embrace forgiveness in all your relationships. Once you start to tell your story, you may discover that you are already further along the path than you realised.

Questions to help you write your own story

When and what have you forgiven?

Think about a time in your life when you have forgiven.

- What did it feel like? How did you know you had forgiven? What changed?
- Did you verbalise your forgiveness or was it an internal change of heart?
- Did you make a conscious decision to forgive? If you did, what sparked that decision?
- Was there anything that you did, or that someone else did, that helped you begin to heal and reach a point where you felt able to forgive?

- Looking back, did you receive help that you did not recognise at the time?
- What can you learn from your own experience of forgiveness? How will you behave differently as a result?

For times when you need to be more forgiving

Sometimes we don't recognise unforgiveness because the feeling isn't tied to one specific offence but emerges under the weight of a thousand small grudges that pile slowly one upon another.

- Are there any areas in your life where you would like to practise forgiveness more readily?

The stories in this book showed lots of practical ways in which people were able to move towards forgiveness. These included accepting help and reaching out in friendship, appreciating the goodness in life, and trying to think about the issue in question from another perspective.

- Can you use any of these examples, or experience from your own life, to help you feel more forgiving? Do you need to change the way that you communicate your needs? What would it mean for you to do that?
- Do you need to hear an apology before you can forgive? What would happen if that apology never came?
- What does unforgiveness feel like? What would it mean to you to be released from the anger and resentment of unforgiveness?
- Are you carrying guilt from something you have done to someone else who refuses to forgive you? Even if you

apologise, you may never hear the words, 'I forgive you,' but how can you act as if you are forgiven? Have you learned from your mistake and changed your behaviour accordingly? If you have violated your own standards, what action do you need to take to make sure that it never happens again? Is there any help that you can get with this?

- Imagine forgiveness as a gift to yourself. What would you need to believe in order to feel that way now? What are you willing to do to make that happen?

Commit to doing one thing differently to help you live a more forgiving life. Write down what that change will be and why you are committed to doing it.

For situations where you feel that you can't forgive

Sometimes we have been hurt so deeply or so often that forgiveness appears impossible. At times like this, we need to be gentle with ourselves and ask, 'Am I being realistic in my expectations of forgiveness? Am I worried that, because forgiveness hasn't happened quickly, I will be unable to forgive?'

At such times, we need to remember that forgiveness is never easy and often it is a struggle. We need to ask for help, and sometimes, when we think that there is nothing we can do, actually there is. We can pray and we can wait. Keep believing for a release from your pain and let the seeds of your intention take root.

Forgiveness is not a weakness. It is a commitment to love and to live the best life that you can. Your story isn't over yet: how it ends is up to you.

Prayer for forgiveness

Dear God, you see all things and know what has happened in my life.

Even when I hide my pain from others, you know that I am hurting and you understand why.

I know that what is done cannot be undone, and I don't ask you for that. I ask for the pain inside me to subside, so that it doesn't overshadow all that is good in my life.

I want to move forward, but I don't know what the future will look like for me. I feel trapped by this hurt.

I don't want past events to stop me from being happy and enjoying my life, but I don't know how this is possible.

Please help me in this, God. I trust you to heal me. Keep me close to you.

Help me to recognise help, however it appears, and to be aware of the strength within me to help myself.

Open my heart and fill it with your love.

I pray that, in time, I will experience your gift of forgiveness, and that your love will shine from me on to others. Amen

WHERE TO FIND HELP

Association of Christian Counsellors
www.acc-uk.org

An umbrella organisation that can put you in touch with a Christian counsellor in your area. It provides a nationwide system for the accreditation of Christian counsellors broadly acceptable to Christian churches, counselling organisations and the wider community, and develops relationships with organisations such as the social services and health authorities, and with professional bodies and church denominations.

Address: 29 Momus Boulevard, Coventry, CV2 5NA
Tel: 0845 124 9569

The Forgiveness Project
www.theforgivenessproject.com

A UK-based charitable organisation that explores forgiveness, reconciliation and conflict resolution through real-life human experience. The Forgiveness Project has no religious or political affiliations.

Address: Forgiveness Project, 42a Buckingham Palace Road, London SW1W 0RE
Email: info@theforgivenessproject.com
Tel: 020 7821 0035

Veterans UK
www.veterans-uk.info

A government agency offering help and advice to anyone who has served in HM Armed Forces, regular or reserve, including National Servicemen, former Polish forces under British command and Merchant Mariners who have seen duty in military operations (for example, the Falklands conflict).

Email advice point: veterans.help@spva.gsi.gov.uk
Helpline: 0800 169 2277
Dedicated helpline staff offering advice on war pensions, Armed Forces compensation scheme, Armed Forces pensions, medals, service records and almost any other matters, such as statutory benefits, money worries, loans and grants, emergency accommodation and employment.

Blind Veterans UK, formerly St Dunstan's
www.blindveterans.org.uk

A charity that gives blind veterans access to the finest quality of services to help them discover life beyond sight loss. This includes practical and emotional support, providing lifelong welfare support, rehabilitation, training, long-term nursing, residential and respite care.

Address: Blind Veterans UK, 12–14 Harcourt Street, London W1H 4HD
Tel: 020 7723 5021

Restorative Justice Council

www.restorativejustice.org.uk

Restorative processes bring into communication those harmed by crime or conflict and those responsible for the harm, enabling everyone affected by a particular incident to play a part in repairing the harm and finding a positive way forward.

Address: Beacon House, 113 Kingsway, London WC2B 6PP
Tel: 020 7831 5700

Prison Fellowship

www.prisonfellowship.org.uk

A network of more than 1,800 volunteers who aim to show Christ's love to prisoners by coming alongside them, praying and supporting them in change. Services are offered to all who request them, regardless of their beliefs.

Address: Prison Fellowship England and Wales, PO Box 68226, London SW1P 9WR
Tel: 020 7799 2500
Email: info@prisonfellowship.org.uk

The Tim Parry, Johnathan Ball Foundation for Peace

www.foundation4peace.org

A UK organisation that supports those affected by conflict, acts of terror and politically motivated violence, to positively contribute to peace.

Address: The Peace Centre, Peace Drive, Great Sankey,
Warrington, WA5 1HQ
Tel: 01925 581231
Email: info@foundation4peace.org

The World Community for Christian Meditation
www.wccm.org

An international community that teaches contemplative
prayer in the form of silent meditation, using the teachings
of Benedictine monk John Main.

Address: The School of Meditation, The World Community
for Christian Meditation, St Mark's Myddelton Square,
London, EC1R 1XX
Email: welcome@wccm.org
Tel: 020 7278 2070.

The Miscarriage Association
www.miscarriageassociation.org.uk

A national charity that provides support and information on
the subject of pregnancy loss.

Address: The Miscarriage Association, 17 Wentworth
Terrace, Wakefield, WF1 3QW
Helpline: 01924 200799
Email: info@miscarriageassociation.org.uk

The Marylebone Centre

www.marylebonecentre.co.uk; www.sexual-addiction.co.uk

The Marylebone Centre provides psychological and psychosexual therapy, specialising in the treatment of personal, sexual and relationship problems.
Address: 79 Marylebone Lane, London, W1U 2PX
Tel: 020 7224 3532
Email: info@marylebonecentre.co.uk

References

1 C.S. Lewis, *The Problem of Pain* (HarperCollins, 2009)
2 Oscar Romero, *The Violence of Love*, trans. James R. Brockman (Orbis, 2004)
3 Mark 8:36 (NLT)
4 Isaiah 55:8
5 Matthew 7:24–27
6 Psalm 137:1–4
7 Luke 22:41–44
8 Ephesians 4:26
9 Matthew 7:3–5

The Recovery of Love

Walking the way to wholeness

Naomi Starkey

Using story, reflection on Bible passages and quotations, the trajectory of the book is from emptiness and despair to certain hope, from confusion through penitence to the great joy of forgiving and receiving forgiveness. A constant theme is the interplay between God's unmerited grace and mercy and our human failings; at the heart of the story is the meaning of love.

The good news that we have been given to share is that the world's hunger for love can be met only in God's neverending embrace. Before that hunger can be understood, however, one question must be pondered and eventually answered: what do we really want?

ISBN 978 1 84101 892 8   £6.99
Available from your local Christian bookshop or, in case of diffi-culty, direct from BRF: please visit www.brfonline.org.uk.

Also available for Kindle.

See overleaf for an extract from this book.

The Recovery of Love

Naomi Starkey

11
The mother: love

The woman is our guide as we walk along the corridor, up a staircase, along another corridor and up a further staircase that brings us to what appears to be the top floor of the house. We reach a narrow landing and ahead is a doorway leading to a long, dimly lit room. At the far end, people are sitting round a low table, talking and laughing quietly together. As we cross the threshold, the warm, drowsy air of the room envelops us. The walls have been painted dark red and are crowded with pictures—paintings, framed photographs, maps—and comfortable armchairs and sofas are arranged across the carpeted floor.

'Have a seat, where you can find one. This is a good place for resting. Resting and reflecting. Remembering, too, if you like.' The woman smiles but her eyes are thoughtful as she looks at us.

Remembering: what might we possibly want to remember from before? The snarling aggression in the city streets, the roaring traffic, the loneliness?

'Anything you want…' she goes on, as if replying to a question, still surveying us carefully. 'Just a thought, though —the more you remember something, the more you bring back the feelings to do with it, the good but also the bad. And some of the bad can be hard to bear, even after a lot of time has passed.

'You see,' she continues, after another moment of reflective silence, 'there is not a single person who does not have memories they treasure but also ones that torment them. And they will have memories that they return to, again and again, to try and understand. What was going on? Why did that happen? What did it all mean? Maybe they imagine that by replaying a scene over and over in their head, the faces and words and gestures will suddenly fall into a pattern that makes sense of everything that happened before and afterwards.'

There is another pause. The people at the far end of the room have fallen quiet now, listening to what the woman is saying.

'You know,' she goes on at last, 'remembering can be very precious because it can bring back something or someone we thought we had lost. As we remember that thing or that person, old, tender feelings can live again, as if no time has passed, as if nothing else has happened. And, sometimes, that is what we need to give us the strength to walk on.'

She walks over to a wooden sideboard, ranged against the dark red wall, and picks up a photo frame.

'Look.' She holds it out towards us—a digital photo display, flashing up a succession of images of a beautiful dark-haired young woman holding a baby, a toddler, a grinning little boy. As we view scene after scene, the rapturous love between them, the delight of mother in son and devotion of son to mother, dazzles: the two of them on the beach, laughing in the rain, dancing, hugging, asleep in each other's arms. Looking at such images, it is hard not to smile, and the woman is also smiling as she looks at them, this time without any reserve in her face.

'Some of you will know,' she says, shaking her head, still smiling. 'There is nothing quite like it—the firstborn, especially if you have longed for that baby's coming, month after month, before you even conceived. And although you know it must happen, it is still a shock when something male comes out of your body. Of course you know it happens, but it still seems the strangest thing when it happens to you! And then that little boy grows into a man, taller and stronger than you, and you look at him and still remember how he once fitted into your lap, top to toe on your knees.

'You look at him, grown, and you know for sure that he is the most handsome, most wonderful son ever born, because he is yours. There is no one else like him in the whole world and never will be again. He is irreplaceable, always.'

She puts down the photo frame, the smile lingering at the corners of her mouth, and when she looks at us again, her gaze is like sunlight. 'Whatever some people may say, I for one think the love is worth any loss.'

❖ ❖ ❖

The angel Gabriel was sent by God to a town in Galilee called Nazareth, to a virgin engaged to a man whose name was Joseph... The virgin's name was Mary. And he came to her and said, 'Greetings, favoured one! The Lord is with you.' But she was much perplexed by his words and pondered what sort of greeting this might be. The angel said to her, 'Do not be afraid, Mary, for you have found favour with God. And now, you will conceive in your womb and bear a son, and you will name him Jesus...' Mary said to the angel, 'How can this be, since I am a virgin?' The angel said to her, 'The Holy Spirit will come upon you, and the power of the Most High will overshadow you; therefore the child to be born will be holy; he will be called Son of God...' Then Mary said, 'Here am I, the servant of the Lord; let it be with me according to your word.'

LUKE 1:26–38 (NRSV, ABRIDGED)

How can we possibly get to grips with this Bible passage, this beyond-extraordinary encounter? All artists, writers, story-tellers and preachers ought to falter here and admit that, in the end, they can only come up with the vaguest of vague impressions, a hopelessly limited 'something like'. Should we imagine the modest recoil of a Raphael virgin, the uncertainty of a Rossetti (go on, look them up online), the stylised pose of an Orthodox icon, or something more homely—a teenage girl in Middle Eastern first-century peasant dress, dropping her water jug as she is startled at the well?

In struggling to understand what happened and what it meant, perhaps we can think of a moment when we felt chosen in some way, as if a hand had reached into our lives, taken hold of us and brought about profound change. If we think long enough, we may be able to call to mind such a point in time (happening to others, if not to us), a pivotal event after which things were never quite the same again.

Why me—or you? Why not me—or you?

God knows the answer to such questions.

Let's stop and try to reason out why the Son of God did

not follow 'divine convention' for his incarnation. In line with the sort of stories told by many of the world's cultures and faiths, he could have chosen to spring fully grown from a suitably suggestive cleft in a sacred mountain or gallop down from heaven on the back of a white elephant. It would surely have been no problem for the Father to shape the Son from a handful of desert sand or even bring him to life—why not?—from a pile of autumn leaves. Instead, Mary was chosen, singled out for all time from every other woman who ever had been or ever would be, chosen as God-Bearer.

There was a father too, of course—Joseph, the role model for fathers everywhere who have had to care for a child not their own. Yet this unusually special son could easily have been a foundling, discovered in a special place after words of special prophecy. He could have been delivered in the arms of an angel, fully formed, to his waiting foster home. But it seems that Jesus needed a birth-mother. He had to be born of a woman, actually partaking of her flesh and blood, nurtured inside her body, suckled by her body, held in her arms, kissed by her, loved.

Why?

It was so, surely, because that gestation, those nine months in a woman's body, and that prosaically natural birth in some mysterious way accelerated the process of redemption, the process that culminated at Calvary and beyond. God himself is born as human, literally embodying salvation. At the point of conception (and it is interesting to speculate whether this happened while the angel was speaking to her, or whether she was already pregnant, or whether she sensed it happening later), God and the image of God merge into one. The incarnation did not happen as a necessary, essentially time-wasting prelude to the crucifixion; it was a bestowing of blessing and divine favour on the world that God had made, on the people created to bear his likeness.

Thus everything, absolutely everything, changes. The realms of time and eternity collide; the furthest parameters of possibility are redrawn to encompass the infinite. But at that pivotal moment of angelic encounter, what we actually see is a young woman standing in bright Middle Eastern sunlight, saying, 'Here am I, the servant of the Lord; let it be with me according to your word.' In that response, accepting with immeasurable grace her status as chosen one, she is herself eternally transfigured, made over into the new Eve for the redeemed creation.

As we look at the new Eve, with the Son of the Most High in her arms, we see a girl cradling her firstborn son, Saviour of the world but none the less her own baby boy. Just as humanity is hallowed by the Creator's choice to humble himself to the status of creature, so the love of a mother for her child is hallowed because God himself partook of it. Considered logically, it would have been much simpler for Jesus to burst on to the scene as an adult, perhaps a wandering preacher appearing from over the sea or out of the wilderness. Being labelled 'the carpenter's son' did not do much for his Messiahship credentials. Even so, for 30 years he lived in his family home, surrounded by his mother's love and care.

Maybe in those quiet 30 years, the Son of God simply enjoyed being loved, with the kind of instinctive love, motherly love, that means the one who loves is prepared to die for the beloved without a second's hesitation, that means she sees beauty and intelligence, potential and achievement, in the beloved where outsiders may struggle to discern anything particularly special. Mary was not chosen as an 'empty vessel', a mere incubator for the divine embryo; she was chosen as his mother. She loved her son and, in loving him, she (like mothers everywhere and across time) thereby taught him something of what love means and what it means to love.

For reflection

'God loves as mothers love—extravagantly, pouring love out without measure. God loves intimately, each one of us as a different person, and equally, every one of us as much as all the others, however many there are.'

TERESA MORGAN, *SEASONS OF THE SPIRIT* (BRF, 2010), P. 47.

12
The friends: love

In the soothing atmosphere of this attic room, remembering starts to feel less risky. When the very air is imbued with safety, we sense that this is somewhere we can truly relax. Here we can think about unpacking (or at least venturing near) some of those memories boxed and stored in the darkest, most spidery corner of our selves. Here, instinct tells us, there will be arms to hold us, if that is what we want, and kindness that is unembarrassed by the free flow of tears.

Not in the mood for tears? No problem.

Let's venture down the room to where the group is seated round the table. These people have been eating and drinking together, enjoying an Indian takeaway and a few bottles of beer, by the looks of things. From the casual intimacy of bodies resting against each other, arms draped around shoulders, it is clear that this is a group of close and trusted friends, both men and women, and so familiar and at ease with one another that they are free of the petty undercurrents of rivalry and flickers of sexual tension that can test the bonds of so many such groups.

As we hesitate on the edge, unsure whether they will welcome company, they notice our presence, they smile, and the circle widens far enough to make room for us. Conversation continues to flow between them and it is clearly up to us to listen and learn when it is appropriate to join in, rather than expecting attention to shift to us.

As we pick up the thread of their talk, it becomes clear that they are remembering together, creating a composite picture out of their shared memories. This picture is illuminated by the love with which they speak, until it is almost as if the one they recall is visibly projected in miniature on the table in the middle of them, a hologram beamed by the heart.

'I used to hope that I was the one closest to him.' It is one of the women speaking. In the dim light of this long room, she looks young-ish, pretty-ish. Her voice sounds young anyway, if a little tired and wistful.

The slightly older woman next to her runs a soothing hand along her friend's arm. 'I think there were times when each of us hoped that.'

'But…'—a man with a straggly, rather half-hearted beard leans across the table towards them to emphasise his point. 'He definitely needed all of us, at different times and in different ways.'

'He needed his own space, too.' The man who speaks now is slighter and his voice much harder to catch than his bearded neighbour's. 'Don't you think he kept a space round him that none of us was allowed into?'

'I used to worry that he might be lonely,' the tired and wistful woman says, tiredly and wistfully.

The straggly-bearded man smiles and reaches out to touch her hand. 'Not lonely. I don't think he was ever lonely. Alone, yes, but that's what he wanted. He was totally his own person.'

It is as if that affectionate, undemanding touch unlocks something in her. Abruptly her face crumples and she tries to swallow the beginnings of a sob. 'It wasn't that I wanted him just for myself. I was just so desperate to make sure that he was happy.

'Then again…' She stops and sighs. 'In so many ways it

was enough, just being with him, and, when I was not with him, knowing that before long I would be with him again.' She looks round the circle of kind faces (let us hope that we look kind, too, and not simply puzzled by this curious discussion). 'You know, I can't imagine feeling such a connection with another person again. Even though—' she breaks off again, gulps, regains control. 'Even though I can't be with him now, I will never, ever stop feeling, well, blessed by what I had then, in that connection. I remember, when he looked at me—'

Her composure disintegrates and the circle of friends responds with hugs and soothing noises. Thus it is that we may be the only ones who notice the words of the softly spoken, slightly built man: 'He looked at me like that, too.'

His eyes are shiny with tears, but the memory makes his smile beautiful.

❖ ❖ ❖

Six days before the Passover Jesus came to Bethany, the home of Lazarus, whom he had raised from the dead. There they gave a dinner for him. Martha served, and Lazarus was one of those at the table with him. Mary took a pound of costly perfume made of pure nard, anointed Jesus' feet, and wiped them with her hair. The house was filled with the fragrance of the perfume.

JOHN 12:1–3

This is one of those Gospel passages that would surely make many people's list of top ten favourite New Testament readings. We see Jesus at ease with his friends and then the lavish anointing, followed by the denunciation of one of the other disciples, shocked by the wanton generosity. As with so many favourite readings, the challenge is how to read it with fresh eyes, to see past a mental tableau of posed figures in quaint costume in a stage-set 'Bible times' home. We can try to imagine it as it would have been, a moment in time when the final outcome of events was unclear, when all kinds of possible futures might have been hovering unspoken in the minds of those present.

We are told elsewhere in the Gospels that Jesus' relationship with his own family was troubled at times, as they struggled to understand what exactly he was up to. Here in Bethany, some two miles from Jerusalem, he could be at rest and receive the love and honour of his three close friends, each expressing that love in their own way. Martha served the guests with food, as was customary for the women of the house; Mary apparently had a tendency to break with convention in an outrageous way. Luke 10:39 records how she once sat with the men to listen to Jesus; here she offers a humiliating and also deeply intimate act of devotion. Only the lowest of the low touched the feet of another; a woman would only uncover and loosen her hair as a sign of love—for her husband—or as a sign of mourning, indicating a total loss of self-respect and dignity in the face of great grief.

Two sisters—one honouring their friend in the traditional way with food and hospitality, the other by a show of love that unforgettably subverted tradition. And their brother—what of Lazarus, identified as one whom Jesus loved, just like 'the beloved disciple' who is so described only in John's Gospel (and traditionally identified as John himself)? It is hard to imagine what could possibly have been going through his mind as he lounged at table with the one who had brought him back from the dead. We can only speculate as to how extraordinary that connection must have been.

Any kind of life-changing event forges links between those involved. The one who saves a life may find that they are bound to the one saved by the latter's debt of gratitude; equally, the one who takes a life is inextricably linked with the one whose life has been taken, and with those left behind to mourn. Whether life-saver or life-taker, that person becomes for ever the pivotal character in a particular drama, without whose intervention everything would have been different.

At the same time, in the person of Jesus we see one who, during his earthly life, did not remain remote from human contact, appearing as *deus ex machina* to dispense wisdom and miracles and then withdrawing into a special heavenly realm. Yes, he needed time apart in the hills to pray, but so do many people. He was not a hermitic figure, like some of the more inscrutable and prickly Desert Fathers, shunning mortal distractions in order to focus as intently as possible on the heavenly realm—or, indeed, like his cousin John, the wild and shaggy desert prophet.

Just as Jesus did not burst into the world fully formed, but was born of a woman and raised by her, thus hallowing a mother's love for her child, so he lived in close and loving relationship with others as an adult. They loved and needed him; he loved and needed them (remember, for instance, his anguish in the garden of Gethsemane, when his friends first fell asleep and then ran off and left him). He hallowed not only the mother–child relationship, as we saw earlier, but also the life-sustaining bonds of friendship—and such friendship means not casual acquaintance or 500-odd 'online friends', but love. We're talking the kind of mutual love where each gives the other what they are able to give, and the other does not selfishly demand what cannot, for whatever reason, be given. It's the kind of love that says, 'We accept each other, look out for each other's interests, welcome each other, strive to understand each other, be there for each other as much as we are able, celebrate our belonging together...' and all this in a way that has the potential to draw in rather than exclude newcomers.

In the context of such relationships, we learn what it truly means to connect with another, not to flatter ourselves ('look who I'm friends with!') but because true connection can bring life, growth and fruitfulness. Freely expressed love, grace and generosity have the power to call forth a corresponding response, as the heaven-sent love, grace and generosity of Jesus warmed those around him and nurtured in them the beginnings of a kinship likeness to him, their friend and brother.

In the context of such relationships, bonds can develop that are strong and grow stronger over time, while remaining flexible enough to last through the harshest of life circumstances. Then, when we meet again, even if it is after many years, the connection is still there, unmistakable.

In the context of such love, many fears can start to be put aside, not least the lurking fear that loss has the last word.

For reflection

'There is only one love, and that is God, who is present, recognised or not, in every love.'

TIMOTHY RADCLIFFE, *WHAT IS THE POINT OF BEING A CHRISTIAN?* (BURNS & OATES, 2005), P. 105

Enjoyed

this book?

Write a review—we'd love to hear what you think.
Email: reviews@brf.org.uk

Keep up to date—receive details of our new books as they happen.
Sign up for email news and select your interest groups at:
www.brfonline.org.uk/findoutmore/

Follow us on Twitter @brfonline

By post—to receive new title information by post (UK only), complete the form below and post to: BRF Mailing Lists, 15 The Chambers, Vineyard, Abingdon, Oxfordshire, OX14 3FE

Your Details
Name _____
Address_____
_____
Town/City _____ Post Code _____
Email_____

Your Interest Groups (*Please tick as appropriate)	
☐ Advent/Lent	☐ Messy Church
☐ Bible Reading & Study	☐ Pastoral
☐ Children's Books	☐ Prayer & Spirituality
☐ Discipleship	☐ Resources for Children's Church
☐ Leadership	☐ Resources for Schools

Support your local bookshop
Ask about their new title information schemes.